TOWARDS THE CLOUDS II

CHRONICLE OF A RESCUE IN THE PATAGONIAN MOUNTAINS

To Leo Ferraris, a poet of the skies.

FOREWORD BY BOB BREEDEN
ILLUSTRATIONS BY PABLO WEGRZYN.

Title: Towards the Clouds II - Chronicle of a Rescue in the Andes
Author: Daniel Roy Wegrzyn
Illustrations: Pablo Wegrzyn

Contact: dwegrzyn@gmail.com

1st Edition
Year of Printing: 2025
ISBN: 9798305270723
Sello: Independently published

Cover Design: Pablo Wegrzyn

INDEX

IN MEMORIAN

I wanted to begin this book with a tribute to Leo Ferraris, to honor his memory and preserve the inspiration he left for those of us privileged to have known him. Leo left us far too soon, and while his passing came as he was doing what he loved most, it created an immense void for his family, friends, and the entire aviation community. Yet, his memory, his legacy, his teachings, and his smile will remain with us forever.

His life was a harmony of passion, dedication, and excellence. Leo lived each moment of his life with intensity, a life marked from his earliest days by the magic of aviation. Surrounded by airplanes as he grew up, it was as if his destiny had always been intertwined with the wind and the heights. He naturally absorbed the same passion that lived within his father, Leandro. His father was not only his mentor and guide but also imparted teachings that transcended the technical complexities of flight. He instilled in Leo a profound and reverent respect for the art of flying, beyond mere skill, transforming it into a philosophy of life.

At first, Leo dreamed of flying above the clouds as an airline pilot, but fate had a more diverse, more colorful path in store for him—one that he embraced with enthusiasm and dedication. It was along this path that he found the ultimate expression of his talent, a versatility that made him stand out in every role he undertook: as a flight instructor, an agricultural pilot, an executive pilot, and above all, as a master of aerobatics.

Aerobatics became his truest language, his purest art. For Leo, the sky was not merely a space to fly; it was a stage on which to express himself with beauty and precision. His flights were much more than demonstrations of technical skill; they were works of art and poetry. Every maneuver carried a lyrical quality, evoking feelings and emotions that amazed those of us watching from the ground.

His creativity knew no bounds. Breaking conventions and barriers, Leo achieved a feat of pure innovation by performing nighttime aerobatics with his Super Decathlon. The aircraft, outfitted with multicolored LED lights, stood out against the darkness, with flashes of color and smoke illuminated by an orange glow reminiscent of a fire-breathing dragon. Those fortunate enough to witness him soaring through starry skies will never forget those magical moments when, under his command, the night air came alive with dazzling lights and breathtaking acrobatics. His flights were not only a display of technical prowess but a spectacle that reached into the soul.

Dedicating this book, Towards the Clouds II, to him is a humble tribute to this exceptional and beloved pilot, who was also an individual of great integrity and generosity. Through this gesture, I hope in some small way to help keep his name alive and preserve the essence of his flights.

Leo, as you now navigate other skies, this book is in your honor. May your free spirit continue to inspire us to reach new heights, both in the air and in life itself.

ACKNOWLEDGMENTS

First and foremost, I want to acknowledge Queque Parodi, whose accident on the snow-covered surface of a frozen lake in the high mountains marked the beginning of this story. His strength, courage, and determination in the face of an extreme situation not only provided the starting point for this narrative but also became a source of inspiration for all of us in the general aviation community, especially those of us who frequently fly in mountainous terrain.

I am deeply grateful to all the friends, pilots, rescuers, and professionals who, from the moment news of the accident reached the aviation community, did not hesitate to set in motion a great mechanism of action. With their knowledge, experience, and teamwork, they contributed with dedication and effort to the search and rescue of Queque.

My utmost appreciation goes to the rescue helicopter pilots, Tomy Bosio and Hernán Fabbio, as well as the logistics team, who were responsible for recovering Queque under marginal conditions. Without their skill, technical expertise, and professionalism, this rescue story would not have been possible. They embody the very best that aviation has to offer.

To Walter Marchand and Martín Mol, the baqueanos from Cholila, who provided invaluable ground assistance and organized a rescue patrol as part of the operation. Their knowledge of the terrain, experience, and willingness to assist in Queque's recovery were instrumental.

To my family, for their constant support and patience with

each of my projects. Especially to my wife, Silvia, who is not only a cornerstone of my life but also continuously supports me in endeavors like this one. She meticulously reviewed the manuscript with her professional, critical, and detailed perspective. To my son, Pablo, whose illustrations enrich this book, bringing this story to life with his creativity and talent. His support and presence elevate the quality of this work.

To Marko Magister, for his valuable insights into the design. His vision and technical perspective were significant contributions that helped refine the presentation of this book and bring the project to its best form.

I also wish to extend my sincere thanks to Edward Macadam, a retired Aerolíneas Argentinas captain and technical aviation English instructor. It is an honor to have his friendship and invaluable support. I hold deep admiration for him, not only as a pilot of great distinction but also as an exemplary individual and a true "gentleman of the skies." His constructive critique of the early drafts, combined with his English-language review, gave me tremendous confidence in the content captured in these pages.

Similarly, I owe genuine gratitude to Günter Schuster, the most senior active pilot in Argentina, who has become my foremost aviation mentor. With each meeting and flight together, I gain lessons that transcend aviation itself. I deeply appreciate the privilege of having him and his wife, Renée, take the time to evaluate the book's content and enrich it with their wise and valuable observations.

To Bob Breeden, one of the most renowned bush pilots in Alaska, repeatedly recognized as a champion in STOL flying competitions.

His generosity in agreeing to write the foreword, after a critical review of the work, has been an incredible honor. His support and validation are a significant encouragement for this project.

To Patricia Cilio, an avid reader and lifelong friend whose connection to aviation is only through our friendship and her brother Gustavo, my dear friend with whom I began my journey into the world of aviation. I deeply value her critical eye and her generosity in reading and correcting my writings. I recall her once telling me she had read Shakespeare in English, which led me to jokingly ask if she could "lower the bar" and read Wegrzyn, thus agreeing to edit this book. I am profoundly grateful for her time and dedication.

Finally, I want to extend my gratitude to everyone who, in one way or another, contributed to bringing this book to life. To all those whose support and commitment made it possible to recount these experiences, with both their successes and their mistakes, in hopes that they may serve as lessons and examples for better decision-making in similar situations.

This book is, above all, a tribute to teamwork and a love for aviation. Thank you all for being part of this story and for helping, through your effort and dedication, to bring this project to fruition. This narrative ultimately seeks to uncover the best within ourselves when faced with adversity, as illustrated by the situations presented here.

PREFACE

By Bob Breeden
Alaska

Questing. Grand Questing. The deep desire to wander and weave through new mountains and country is perhaps a most basic explorer's mindset. Why? Perhaps it is there, in pristine natural beauty, that a person's soul finds sanctuary, a sanctuary of both enchanting delight and gracious peace. Flying, with it's risks and rewards into such wilderness country is often the best and only way to quest deeply.

Experience. Honed, intricate with thousands of points of reference to draw from to manage a challenging environment. Winds, or no wind at all. Or wind to come, unseen. But are there telltale markers aforehand? Visibility. Is the light brilliantly clear from high above in late Spring or Summer, or low angle off-season and occluded by shadow or clouds above? With height come the cold at height elevations, sometimes even colder because of cold air falling off of mountains even higher. This cold is in stark contrast to the more habitable place recently departed from, and initially can come as quite a surprise.

Snow condition. Would it be benign if a tire were to touch and run along on the surface, as on a smooth beach, or had I better stay at a height that will prevent any possibility of that occurrence? Is the snow firm, settled, wind hardened, or recent cold fluff that can't be felt until it draws me in? These are just a few of the many aspects to manage, and the matrix of them when all are present at the same time is especially a concern. And, with all it's beauty, the mountain doesn't care if you regard it's challenges properly or not.

Judgement. With that depth of experience, comes judgement. Judgement brings healthy fear when the margins of what is known to be safe are pushed upon – and with higher levels of judgement, these fears develop with the idea of being out of a comfort zone of reasonable winds, good visibility, or proper dress for the cold are even contemplated. This fear can vanish instantly when a pilot knowingly guides away from the dangers. Empirically, well-homed judgement comes from a vast array of experiences to draw from. It is judgement that guides travel to the very same place either a comfortable venture or an immensely challenging journey.

Adventure. When at the limit of questing, experience and judgement, comes visceral adventure. Earnest Shackleton didn't expect to lose his ship when he left England for Antarctica. Queque didn't expect not to be able to fly his plane home that day he left Trevelin. This is perhaps the most personally instructive form of experience. Those of us who have been deeply in shock by such difficult experience, but managed this shock and escaped with our lives know what this is. And with appreciation to friends willing to be there when needed most. Queque now joins that elite group of pilots who knows to his core the true severity of questing to fly in the mountains. It is truly beautiful that this is was a successful outcome – that he escaped with this life.

From this adventure, and the new judgement earned, after this bit of rest to let the mental shock wear off, Queque, Dany and Pablo will spend many years in the joy of flying and safely landing in nature's sanctuary. They have the cutting edge mindset now to calmly be able to reach the prettiest places on Earth.

Danny's remarkable achievement in being both part

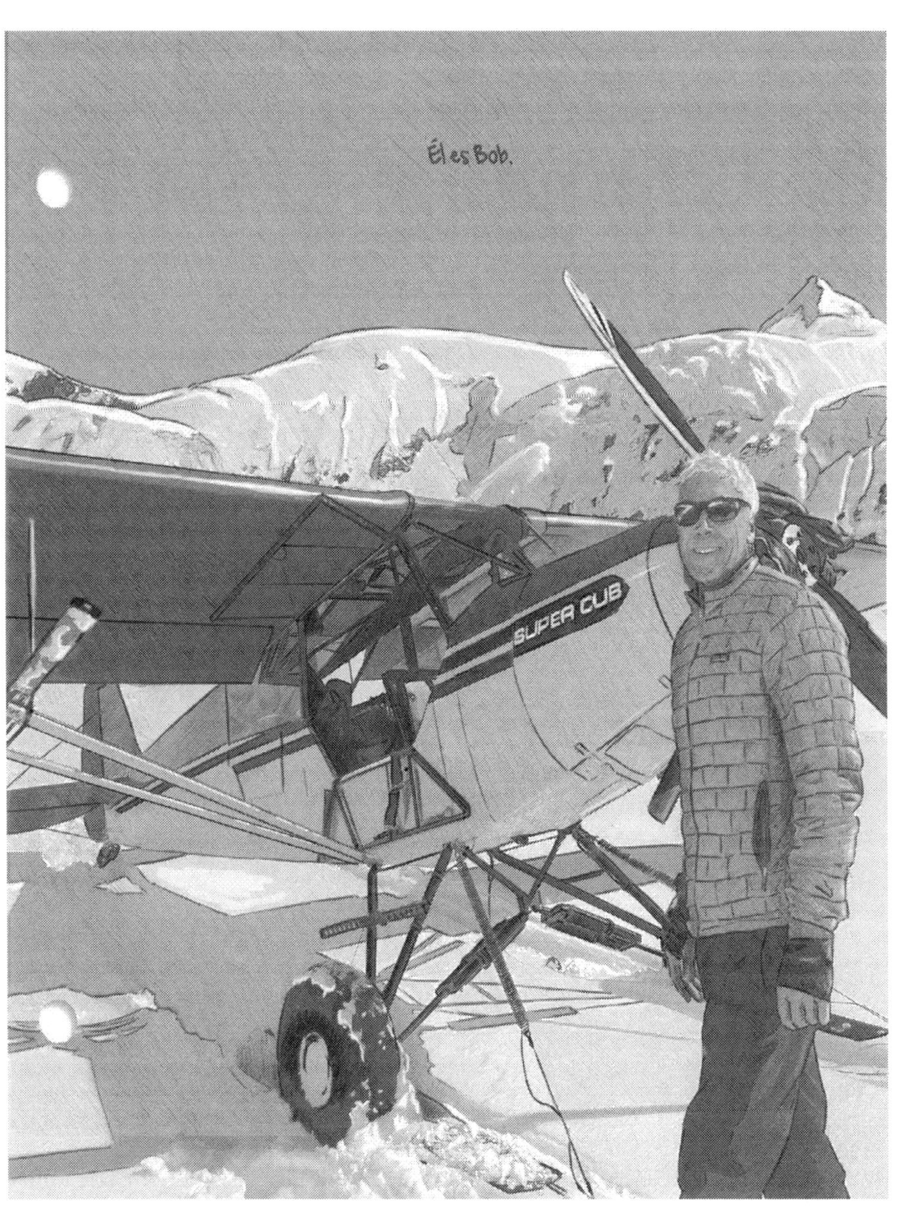
Él es Bob.
SUPER CUB

of and organizing Queque's rescue under very challenging conditions, with limited time for survival in the cold and wind, is commendable. Danny's lifelong knowledge of flight, the people he knew to call upon for the rescue, his understanding of the terrain, and his ability to navigate bureaucratic friction were all essential and exemplary. His story, told here, is magnificent.

INTRODUCTION

Entering the emergency room at the Italian Hospital in Buenos Aires was very uncomfortable. Although the waiting room was crowded, I was attended to with great diligence. I felt a deep discomfort, barely able to muster any strength, and my wife took on the task of holding and accompanying me throughout. It had only been a day since my return to our rural home in Lobos, in the province of Buenos Aires, after a long and arduous journey from Trevelin, in Chubut.

The flight in the Cessna 180 from distant Patagonia—a journey we usually enjoy immensely—had turned into a kind of ordeal. I lacked the strength to control the aircraft, so my son Pablo had to take over, showing remarkable stoicism as he endured not only the entire flight, overcoming fatigue, but also the intense acrid smell from my sickness, as we were both confined in the cramped space of that small cockpit.

At the hospital, the succession of tests and transfers from one area to another was accompanied by a series of questions that were faithfully repeated each time, asking me the same details that were clearly noted at the foot of my gurney. Without realizing at that moment that they were trying to determine if I was oriented in time and space, I decided to answer differently in response to yet another round of questions. In a solemn tone, giving it as much epic weight as I could muster, I explained that I was a Patagonian pilot who had just experienced a difficult situation: the plane accompanying my flight had crashed in the mountains, landing and flipping over on a frozen lake covered in snow; its pilot had spent the night in the mountains, and I had taken on the responsibility of coordinating his search and rescue. I told them it was precisely that—the stress endured, the harsh Patagonian winter, and the poor camp food—that had brought me here, to this hospital bed.

A skeptical silence fell over the room; I could see in their eyes just how implausible my story sounded, especially in a hospital in the center of Buenos Aires, more than 2,000 kilometers from the incident. Before they dismissed it as delirium, one of the doctors, with a look of recognition, mentioned he had read something about it in a newspaper, and as I shared more details, the story began to gain credibility. For a moment, I felt a sense of satisfaction, as if my suffering had a purpose—that it was the price paid for what we had achieved with the rescue team, that the discomfort was worth enduring in exchange for the outcome we'd secured.

But to my disappointment, just when I felt content that what was happening was a consequence of my efforts, they told me that although my experience could have triggered it, it wasn't directly related to what I'd been through. It was something that could have happened at any time, whether I was braving the harsh Patagonian weather or watching a movie in my living room. The tests showed that a tiny stone had obstructed a bile duct, and all it took was removing it to return to normal.

Yet I realized that recounting the story was a release, a kind of catharsis, and that was the moment I decided to write this book. It's based on a real situation, centered on an experience we lived through, as witnesses and protagonists: the accident of Ezequiel "Queque" Parodi, his strategies to survive in the mountains, and the efforts involved in his rescue.

The mountain has always been more than just a landscape; it embodies a challenge of self-overcoming. Approaching it awakens feelings of humility and wonder. Its imposing presence demands respect, and in its silence, it conveys profound knowledge about human limits. For a mountaineer, ascending its steep slopes means facing personal weaknesses and doubts, while reaching the summit represents a personal triumph. Attaining the peak goes beyond physical achievement; it symbolizes the culmination of a process of self-discovery and mental and emotional fortitude.

For a pilot, flying in the mountains, beyond the adventure, technique, and mastery of the aircraft, is an experience that awakens a deep sense of smallness in the face of the vastness of peaks, glaciers, and rock formations. From his privileged position in the airspace, he explores places from a perspective and access impossible to achieve by other means, and he becomes more aware of his vulnerability and insignificance.

Each flight is a reminder of human fragility before nature. The pilot knows that there can be no mistakes. Every maneuver requires precision and, at the same time, a careful instinct for observation. The reflections of light, the shadows cast on the snow, the snowfields, and the clouds hugging the peaks create an impressive scene, igniting a blend of admiration and awe that transforms each flight into a contemplative act.

This book is born out of a passion for mountain flying, and within its pages, in addition to exploring the science and skill of flying over the Patagonian Andes, I narrate a true story that may serve as both a warning and an inspiration. It also stands as a testament to human fragility and strength in the face of the unexpected. In the background, it describes an event of endurance and courage, while revealing the existence of skills, decisions, and acts of survival that can mean the difference between life and death.

In the southern winter, Queque Parodi faced a situation that would mark his life as a pilot due to an accident on Cerro Plataforma, between Cholila and El Bolsón—a place that for many is just a location on the map, but for him has become a landmark. In the midst of the flight, and without prior warnings, he was forced to make an emergency landing on a frozen lagoon, trapped in a relentless geography seemingly designed more to preserve solitude than life.

That night, Queque Parodi had to face something far more intimidating than the cold and the darkness: he had to confront himself, his fears, and the uncertainty of whether he would make it out alive. For hours that felt endless, he was completely alone, enveloped by a silence that only the mountain can offer—a silence that becomes both company and test. His story, intertwined with mountain flying techniques, becomes a lesson on the physical and psychological limits of the human being. Beyond mere chronicle, it serves as a reference to understanding the role that resilience and the ability to adapt to extreme conditions play in aviation.

For me, this experience also marked a turning point. As the person responsible for organizing and executing his rescue, I faced the urgency and complexity of coordinating an operation under conditions where every step, every decision, seemed to either bring us closer or push us further from finding him safe.

Recounting it in these pages is not only about narrating a personal experience, but also about highlighting the commitment and professionalism of those people—pilots and rescuers—who, driven by a deep sense of responsibility, strove, dedicated their time, and gave everything they had, even when facing the risks of the mountains, to search for a fellow pilot, a lost friend.

Pilots who specialize in mountain flying know that it's not just about skill; it involves a relationship with the landscape, a sort of understanding with the mountains, valleys, and winds that travel through every corner of the range. Mountain flying technique encompasses precise maneuvers, a constant assessment of the weather, shifting winds, and the condition of the terrain. But at its core, it's something much more fundamental: a respect for nature and a commitment to safety, knowing that each takeoff, each journey, and each landing carry an inherent risk. Queque Parodi's story reminds us that no manual can foresee everything, and ultimately, true knowledge comes from experience and the ability to improvise, solve, and overcome the unexpected.

Throughout this book, in addition to exploring techniques and strategies that may be useful for other pilots venturing into the mountains, some psychological and emotional aspects of facing adverse flying conditions are highlighted. Parodi's story and his night in the snow under the southern sky is not just a story of accidents and rescues, but of the feelings and thoughts that emerge in those moments of absolute solitude. His experience serves as a reminder that while technology and preparation are essential, the human factor and the ability to adapt to extreme situations remain the core of the experience of navigating these skies.

This book, then, is not meant to be an exhaustive technical guide; it is more a tribute to the spirit of the mountain pilot, to his ability to prepare, face, and overcome the challenges that nature presents in these settings. Ultimately, it is an invitation to all those who seek to understand not only the art of flying, but also the value of life itself when these limits arise and confront us.

ORÍGINS

Millions of years ago, in the depths of a vast ocean, two colossal tectonic plates floated atop the Earth's seething magma. At one point, these plates began to shift and collide, releasing inconceivable forces that shook the planet's foundations. The rock groaned, the ground trembled, and in a dance of fire and destruction, the Earth unleashed a fierce volcanism that illuminated the surface with streams of lava, while rivers of molten rock flowed and cascaded, forming a curtain of ash that darkened the atmosphere.

The Nazca Plate, driven by the unyielding force of subduction, slid beneath the South American Plate, which began to twist, fold, and rise in giant waves of stone. With each push, the land rose in a metamorphosis of solid rock that defied the laws of permanence. Under this intense pressure, the depths became an ocean of liquid rock that, seeking cracks and fissures, exploded upward through volcanic peaks, dispersing in colossal eruptions. Thus, layer upon layer of lava and ash was deposited and solidified, building the ground on which the first elevations took shape.

In that contrast between chaos and order, between violent cataclysms and synchronized chaos, between destruction and creation, from these indomitable forces of creation emerged the imposing, beautiful Andes mountain range.

Over the centuries, the first peaks transformed into colossal formations of rock and snow, a mountain chain growing and expanding, stretching like the spine of an immense petrified dragon. From the warm lands of the tropics to the icy reaches of Patagonia, the Andes rose as a formidable natural barrier. Winds sculpted their summits and cliffs, while snow began to accumulate at their heights, giving birth to glaciers that later fed rivers and lakes, flowing east and west, connecting the Atlantic and Pacific oceans in a network of life and energy.

With the glaciations came new changes: vast rivers of ice descended from the mountains, carving deep valleys and displacing massive rocks. These glaciers carved out canyons and formed ancient lakes, shaping the landscape through a slow but relentless process that defined the current geography. Today, every valley and every mountain is a relic of those glacial eras, a reminder of the forces that sculpted this wild land.

The Andes mountain range remains alive and in constant transformation, still breathing like a sleeping giant. Sometimes, the earth shakes and the mountains murmur, reminding us that this tectonic collision has yet to finish shaping its peaks. The volcanoes, guardians and outlets of subterranean energy, stand as active vents, capable of releasing the accumulated forces from deep within the earth at any moment.

But the Andes are more than rock and ice. As light, temperature, and humidity conditions stabilized, life began to cling to this land. In the tropical zones, biodiversity flourished in complex and lush forms, while in the south, where the climate is harsher, adapted species thrived at their own pace. Moisture-laden winds from the Pacific ascend the slopes, finding cooler temperatures that condense the water into rain or snow, falling on both sides of the mountain range. This moisture gave rise to forests and jungles, which embrace the mountains, anchor the soil, and provide refuge for wildlife, absorbing carbon and oxygenating the atmosphere, creating a delicate balance among land, water, and air.

In this extraordinary setting, we fly, rising into the southern sky and gazing at the mountain range from a privileged perspective. The mountains, sculpted by time and the forces of nature, unfold before our eyes, their secrets revealed with every flight. For Patagonian pilots, navigating these skies is much more than a route; it is a transcendent experience that connects us to the wild essence of the land.

With every flight over the Andes, we pilots feel how the indomitable spirit of Patagonia surrounds us, leaving an indelible mark on our being. This landscape of contrasts, of towering mountains, serene lakes, and ancient forests, reminds us of nature's unbreakable strength and the eternal spirit of the Andes. Flying over this land is an embrace of vastness, a sense of belonging to a story that transcends humanity, revealing at every step the untamed beauty and unyielding power of Patagonia.

CHAPTER 1
MOUNTAIN FLYING

Preparations for the Flight

"Is this flight confirmed, finally?"

Ezequiel "Queque" Parodi answered yes, although it had not yet been validated from LZA, a mountain airstrip where two couples who were the site's custodians awaited the internet satellite connection Elon Musk had recently activated for Argentina.

"It's going to change their lives. They'll be well connected, able to watch TV, take online courses, watch movies—all that up there in the middle of nowhere. But I have to bring the equipment today, as a polar wave is coming in that will likely cover the airstrip with snow."

On my end, I needed to connect the camera located at the airstrip's edge to the internet. I needed it to schedule flights and assess weather conditions before departure.

Aside from the Starlink antennas, Queque needed to bring an implement for the small tractor on the property: a mechanical shovel to remove snow if it accumulated on the airstrip. My presence there and the availability of the C180 offered him the opportunity to transport this tool, too bulky and heavy for the small Piper PA-18.

We prepared both planes. Pablo, my son, removed the rear seats, and we secured the shovel, which took up most of the space, tying it firmly to the plane's floor with a thin but sturdy rope.

With everything ready, we awaited flight confirmation. Although the day had advanced considerably, we estimated we had enough time to go and return with a bit of a cushion, though we'd need additional time on site to install the antennas and run the necessary tests.

It was one of the shortest days of the year—just 9 hours and 3 minutes. Midwinter in the Southern Hemisphere, with days that had been extremely cold and stormy, covering the mountains with snow. But that Monday, July 1, there was a window of good weather.

Once we got the green light, Queque took off right away. His plane was slower, and he had technical work to do at his destination. His other plane, the Cessna 172 XP, had suffered propeller damage while flying along the Atlantic coast of Chubut just two weeks prior. His skill and training had allowed him to make a safe emergency landing on a beach, but he couldn't take off from there and had to wait for a rescue vehicle to tow it to the nearest workshop.

Financial pressure and the need to repair his work plane, which was still out of service, pushed him to complete that day's flight. He needed the money.

We took our time, with no rush, mindful of the importance of this flight, which, practically speaking, was a test. The Cessna 180 had been out of commission for six months, and this was a good opportunity to ensure it was ready for the long journey ahead of us. The next day, or as soon as the weather granted us a safe window, we'd take off from Trevelin, bound for Lobos in the province of Buenos Aires.

Beyond the test and the task at hand, I was also excited to fly among the mountains again, to land once more on the LZA airstrip, where for several years I did the same work Queque now did. I had also planned to land in Cholila, but I had to cancel that plan due to the limited daylight. It would have been different if we'd left early in the morning.

The Cessna 180 touching down its wheels on the Patagonian snow

In my current home, in the vast and flat province of Buenos Aires, nostalgia for the mountains is a constant in my new life. I long to see the land rise into glacier-crowned peaks, towering giants that drain into streams and give birth to lakes, all surrounded by lush forests. I miss that landscape, which, wherever it stretches, creates a scene of sublime beauty.

Therefore, the takeoff from Trevelin marked not only the beginning of a short flight but also an opening into a deep memory, to that seemingly hidden dimension that, with a single visual stimulus, emerges powerfully, unearthing memories, unfolding experiences, and sensations in a web of renewed intensity. Every corner of the landscape became a mirror reflecting memories, turning that flight over the mountainous scene into an introspective journey along familiar paths of geography, bringing back images and stories from not-so-distant times I hadn't thought I'd relive.

The plane çlimbed smoothly at a good rate well-supported by the calm, cold air that day. Below, the flat ground and the surface world grew distant as we set course north over the Percey River valley. And there, in the distance, the familiar contours of the Rivadavia Range began to appear: Cerro La Torta, and farther off, with its imposing presence, the Dos Picos and Tres Picos mountains, standing tall like visible markers, pointing toward Lake Cholila.

The Patagonian mountains have a relatively recent geological history, and erosion has yet to smooth and round them, leaving them with sharp ridges, pronounced peaks, and steep slopes, making them both intimidating and beautiful.

As we continued, we gradually fell silent, savoring this process of recollection in our quietness, captivated by the wintry landscape—a limited palette of few colors, but arranged with precision and exquisite mastery. The glaciers, thickened by the increased snowfall, the bare, gray forests, and the lakes turned emerald green by the melting ice created a scene in which we were mere tiny figures flying above this vastness. Not just spectators of this masterpiece, we were immersed in it.

Before departure, we managed to communicate with Queque, who was en route and informed us that he would follow the Percey River valley toward Cholila, rather than skirting Los Alerces National Park.

Mountain flying never follows a direct route. The rugged and elevated terrain alters the path and forces pilots to choose alternative routes depending on circumstances and the length of the journey. The pilot must use judgment based on the prevailing weather, anticipating that it may change quickly along the way. The pilot also needs to consider the ground elevation, which is closely linked to the aircraft's power availability, determining whether it can safely clear the elevations or if they need to be circumvented. Additionally, the pilot must rely on terrain knowledge to plan the route, especially making safety considerations. Some routes reveal steep areas, while others offer flatter places with potential emergency landing zones.

The estimate given by the GPS didn't match the reality of navigation, as it didn't account for the necessary twists and turns. Nevertheless, we used it because it's an extremely helpful tool for pinpointing one's location, especially valuable when visibility is reduced. Flying in the mountains is like flying among obstacles, and having an exact indication of position, given by the map on the screen and terrain alerts, provides some level of security, even though no one should fly in such conditions.

Once, Queque encountered clouds that led him to the wrong canyon, entering one that closed off. He has a habit of filming all his flights from the cockpit, and it's impressive to watch the 180-degree turn he had to make, almost at the edge of stalling. What saved him was his iPad connected to a GPS antenna and his skill in handling such situations.

I also remember my own experience. During the great forest fire in Cholila, I was flying over the Alerce River, the main tributary of the Tigre River and the largest contributor of water to Lake Cholila. I was flying very low over the terrain when the wind shifted suddenly, trapping me in smoke. I couldn't see forward, only downward, but I had an Aera 500 GPS—quite underestimated in the aviation world—that saved my life. Its low-resolution screen guided me along the valley until I emerged over the lake, where it felt as if someone had drawn back a curtain, instantly clearing the smoke.

Mountain flying comes with greater risks than other types of flight, which is why safety considerations are extremely important, including knowing the aircraft, its power, limitations, speed, and capacity for tight turns, as well as understanding the terrain, weather patterns, and other relevant factors. It's very different from flying over the plains, with a horizon laid out in a straight, uniform line, laminar winds, more predictable weather, and a more regular surface below, offering better emergency landing options.

The primary cause of mountain flying accidents is lack of foresight, compounded in many cases by inexperience, lack of skill, use of unsuitable aircraft, and often adverse weather.

Aircraft Condition

"Danny, you shouldn't tie the tail skid with baling wire! This is unacceptable and penalizable in aviation!"

The person scolding me was Sebastián Jelusic, head of the aeroworkshop in Comodoro Rivadavia, where the annual inspection had to be done. It was difficult to explain to him that I was in the middle of the countryside and, when the cables came loose, the material I had in abundance was that. And he still hadn't seen the upper hinges of the doors, which had come unsoldered due to the roughness of the runways and had been tied together with slings behind the controls, or the wheelbarrow wheel I had placed on the tail skid, which I had found at a hardware store in the town of El Bolsón and fit perfectly on the small rim.

On one of my first flights to La Esperanza airstrip, I was accompanied by Luis Tito Tagle, a knowledgeable person in the area and a fly-fishing guide. On this occasion, he had to assess the fishing situation in the lake and the river flowing from the large body of water.

We had taken off from Cholila carrying cargo. Since the load was quite heavy, and given that the weather was friendly for flying and the distance to cover wasn't much, I reduced the aircraft's fuel load to lighten its weight.

Once the day's tasks were completed, we took off back to Cholila. The aircraft, without rear seats, without cargo, and with little fuel, climbed quickly. But shortly after leveling off, the windshield on the pilot's side started to get smeared with oil. I thought for a moment that the oil filler cap had come loose, or that the dipstick had been improperly secured and had come off. At the same time, I began to evaluate the situation, and the first reasonable alternative that came to mind was to return to

La Esperanza, the nearest airstrip. However, not having oil to replenish would mean leaving the plane behind and descending on foot or horseback. I would then need to return the same way, carrying the oil in a backpack.

I decided to push on a bit further, monitoring temperature and pressure. If I managed to cross into the Tigre River valley, I had enough altitude to glide down to our airstrip located on the other side of the lake.

The plane responded and stayed within normal parameters, although my windshield was now completely covered. I also noticed oil on the side, obscuring the side window. Tito looked at me with some unease but didn't dare say anything. I didn't show visible concern, and he trusted me. We had flown together many times, and in his view, I was executing the best possible operation under the circumstances.

We reached the lake's tip, and except for the mess caused by the oil, the plane flew as if under normal conditions. I reduced power to the minimum and descended gently without stopping the engine, maintaining 80 miles per hour, which, according to the manual, was the best speed for an efficient glide ratio.

I knew a trick taught to me by my glider instructor, César "Gitano" Martínez, which was very useful for estimating glide distance. It involves fixing a point on the windshield and another on the ground and coordinating them with the position of the eye. If the ground point rises, it indicates you won't reach it. If it lowers, you're overshooting and should find another point until they align, marking a fairly accurate path and point of arrival. I genuinely tried to apply it, but the windshield was so smeared with oil that it was impossible.

However, I knew the plane, had sufficient altitude, and kept the engine running in case additional thrust was needed. The oil pressure remained normal, and the temperature had dropped due to the power reduction.

The wind was calm, so I made a direct final approach from the lake, opened my side window, and managed a reasonably good landing by looking out the side of the airstrip.

We taxied to the hangar, and the first thing I did was inspect the cause of the leak. The cap was correctly placed, and the dipstick was in position. I measured the oil and still had eight quarts, well above the manual's limit for the engine. But the image of the oil-smeared plane magnified the situation.

Curious and suspecting a more severe failure, I proceeded to remove the cowling, and the problem became immediately evident, as did the culprit—me.

Back then, the plane was neglected. Both cowling covers had a series of common sheet metal screws for securing them, which would constantly loosen and fall out. For that reason, I always kept several replacements in the ashtray on the right-hand panel. The holes were of various diameters, so my screws also varied in size. The issue arose when I used a particularly long one, which began to rub against the valve cover of one of the cylinders, eventually perforating it and causing the oil to escape.

Not knowing how to fix this, I turned to my father, who happened to be in Cholila. I explained what had happened, and he said he would fix it right away. In Cholila? With almost no tools? I couldn't see any solution other than ordering the replacement part from a workshop. Yet soon after, he appeared whistling one of his favorite tunes, "El Pájaro Chogüí," a song he loved for its connection to the native bird of Argentina's northern jungles and its message of freedom, hope, and resilience in the face of life's adversities.

In his hands were two "extra-large" tubes of a well-known two-component adhesive and a steel wool pad. He removed the cover, cleaned it with gasoline, let it dry, and patched the hole using the paste and the steel wool as reinforcement. I must admit, it worked beautifully. While it took some time to source the replacement part, I was able to fly normally in the meantime.

Perhaps the accumulation of experiences, the inevitable passage of time, and the growth of my survival instinct have gradually shaped my perspective on aviation and, especially, on mountain flying. Having been a witness and participant in various complex and, at times, dangerous situations has left a mark, leading me to adopt a more cautious and prudent approach to this practice. And this is not only to ensure my own safety but also to help mitigate risks for other aviators who share this activity, including my son—a pilot who enjoys flying in mountainous areas and who I deeply hope never has to go through some of the situations I've faced.

An aircraft that flies in the mountains must be in optimal condition. In most flying conditions, even on clear and calm days, it may require the full extent of its power and maneuverability. The plane cannot afford to fail.

Argentina's single-engine aircraft fleet has an average age of 40 years. There are many old planes, sometimes poorly maintained. Our own Cessna 180 is from 1955, and for a time, I had neither a hangar nor enough money to properly maintain it. Beyond age, what weighs most in an aircraft's longevity is its flight time and mode of operation, as well as the care it receives. This

Cessna, even being so old, had no record of any major overhaul in its history before I started using it, though the engine was already due for one.

I flew several hundred hours before opening the engine and replacing the worn parts. Looking back, and considering the type of flights I did, it was very risky not to have done this sooner. My youth, a strong desire to fly, and inexperience at the time led me to surpass several minor incidents, thanks to the plane's reliability and sheer luck.

Flight safety, especially in a small aircraft, depends largely on the reliability and maintenance of its single engine and the structural integrity of the aircraft. Many pilots rely solely on workshops for their aircraft's care, and indeed, aviation regulations do not allow non-professionals to carry out repairs without being a certified mechanic or operating in an authorized workshop.

In fact, the Argentine Civil Aviation Regulations (RAAC) establish rules for the maintenance, repair, and alteration of civil aircraft, specifying that only certified mechanics, technicians, or aeronautical engineers with current licenses, supported by an aeroworkshop, and with a certificate of competency for the type of aircraft they will repair, can intervene. All this must always be certified by ANAC, the National Civil Aviation Authority.

Additionally, all repairs and maintenance activities must be recorded in the engine and airframe logs, detailing the work performed, signed by the responsible technicians, using approved parts and certified as suitable for aviation use.

Furthermore, aircraft inspections are mandated at intervals based on flight hours, calendar time, or a combination of both. These inspections are essential to maintaining airworthiness, ensuring aircraft safety.

Typical inspections based on flight hours, following standard practices and regulations like those of the FAA (Federal Aviation Administration) in the United States, and similar protocols applied by ANAC in Argentina, include a 50-hour inspection—a basic routine check primarily used for oil changes, filter cleaning, or replacement—and a 100-hour inspection, often aligning with the annual inspection, as this is the average flight time for a civil aircraft not used for instruction.

Manufacturers also recommend a "general overhaul," also known as an "overhaul," a comprehensive review and restoration of the engine to ensure its safety and functionality. This is usually required every 1,500 to 2,000 flight hours or every 12 years. In many cases, especially with recurrent misuse, significant issues may be detected, such as loss of compression, excessive wear of internal components, oil leaks, or contaminants in the oil, which may necessitate an early overhaul.

In addition to regular maintenance, Airworthiness Directives (ADs) occasionally arise, which are mandatory orders aimed at addressing safety issues related to aircraft, engines, propellers, and other aeronautical components.

These ADs can be corrective or preventive, issued in response to identified issues through incident reports, routine inspections, data analysis, or technical studies that may point to structural weaknesses or unreliable components.

There are reputable workshops in Argentina with long-standing experience, certified mechanics, and capable staff. However, some workshops capitalize on the complexity and bureaucracy of the maintenance process, placing more emphasis on certification than on the actual mechanical work. Certified aeronautical workshops must meet a series of regulatory requirements and obtain ANAC approval. This certification is crucial for their operation and to ensure they can perform maintenance on registered aircraft. Some workshops use this bureaucratic complexity and certification as added value, promoting regulatory and normative compliance as their main competitive advantage.

Yet many owners, like several aerial applicator pilots, trust more in their own work or that of a highly skilled, though uncertified, mechanic to handle repairs or maintenance. Later, a workshop may lend or provide its signature for an additional fee. This practice is declining as more workshops become available across the country.

But the pilot who operates an aircraft regularly has the best knowledge of its condition. Beyond everything stated above, the most crucial inspection is the pre-flight one, allowing the pilot to identify mechanical, structural, or system issues before they become in-flight failures. This includes detecting fuel leaks, low oil levels, and damage to control surfaces, among other things.

Often, pilots, in their eagerness to fly or to make the most of their time, overlook the importance of this step. However, it's essential to view it as a part of the flight itself, even enjoying it as a prelude to what lies ahead.

While this is closely related to accident prevention—since detecting and correcting problems before takeoff through proper ground inspection can avoid in-flight emergencies—it also affects confidence. A pilot who has performed a thorough pre-flight inspection can be more assured of the aircraft's condition, contributing to a smoother and more focused operation during the flight.

Every aircraft comes with a manual, which is mandatory to carry along with the rest of the documentation. Some airports, where traffic is light, may request it to exercise maximum control. In that manual, there is a section dedicated to pre-flight inspection, presented as a checklist specific to the aircraft. It's extremely useful to ensure that no step is skipped during the inspection.

This checklist mandates a systematic and orderly inspection, generally beginning with the exterior of the aircraft, making a complete circuit and checking the condition of the ailerons, rudder, elevators, and flaps, ensuring they are free from damage and move freely. It includes checking the condition of the wheels, lug nuts, and safety pins, tire pressure, brakes, and landing gear structure. The list indicates that doors and windows should open and close properly.

Before moving the aircraft, it's important to drain the tanks to remove condensation water or identify foreign particles in the fuel. Using inadequate jerry cans for manual fueling and the lack of an effective filter can often dirty the fuel tanks.

Fuel quantity should be verified manually in addition to using the indicators. Most aircraft have a graduated ruler in the seat pocket for a reliable reading.

It's also crucial to check that fuel caps are properly sealed. Many accidents have occurred due to an improperly closed cap or the unintentional oversight of placing it, significantly reducing range. Normally, these aircraft store fuel in their wings, with the cap located on top, so the airflow over the upper surface creates considerable suction that can empty the tank quickly. In aircraft where the fuel selector allows a "both" position, suction in the open tank draws fuel from the other. In such cases, it's important to select the tank with the leak until it's exhausted, keeping the other as reserve.

The engine is checked through inspection covers or by

removing the cowling if easily detachable to detect oil leaks, clamps, spark plug tightness, belt tension, and ensure nothing is loose. Check the oil level, secure the dipstick and filler cap, ensure magnetos are grounded, the mixture and master switch are off, and turn the propeller several times to check compression, lubricate the cylinders for startup, and ensure it's firmly secured. Also, verify the battery's condition and alternator function.

Before boarding, ensure all safety equipment is onboard, including fire extinguishers and other emergency equipment, and that they are present and in good condition.

For mountain flights, it's very helpful to carry a survival kit with essential items for making fire, communication, a personal locator, a sleeping bag, first aid kit, knife, flashlight, and, without overloading, a light set of thermal clothing. In case of an emergency landing in a remote location, these items could mean the difference between life and death. Before each flight, some chocolate, cereal bars, or survival candies can be added. An orange-colored waterproof item is also useful for making a bivouac or drawing attention for a potential rescuer. A detailed kit adapted to our Patagonian region is provided in part IV of this book.

Once in the cockpit, and after starting the engine, make sure all flight and navigation instruments are working correctly, check the flight controls—not only their freedom of movement but also a visual inspection. Also, check the flaps, ensuring they move freely and lock at each position.

Ensure communication systems work correctly, test the radios and other communication equipment, and once the engine is ready, conduct the test according to the manual's instructions.

Pilot Condition

"Queque needs to relax a bit; he's feeling overwhelmed." It was a phrase often heard around the Trevelin airfield.

The truth is that Queque embodies the typical profile of an extremely entrepreneurial person—proactive, with a tremendous drive to seek out opportunities and tackle projects, some of which are challenging to execute. He approaches these projects with creativity and innovation, constantly generating ideas, seeking challenges, and solving situations that others view as very complex with originality.

Entrepreneurship isn't easy, and it often involves facing setbacks and failures. Yet, entrepreneurs have the resilience to recover from failure, learn from it, and move forward with renewed determination. This ability to adapt and persevere in the face of adversity often makes the difference between success and failure.

Another distinctive trait of entrepreneurs is their passion and conviction for what they do, which provides the energy and motivation to set goals and tackle numerous challenges with a vision that goes beyond what others see. They know they face risks and obstacles that are difficult to overcome. However, the key difference between an entrepreneur and someone who isn't is that the former sees clearly what lies beyond each barrier and turns it into a stepping stone toward their goal. This is a strong results orientation, focused on achieving concrete, measurable accomplishments, with a clear horizon and an efficient approach to reaching it, always keeping the final objective in mind.

This approach has earned Queque recognized leadership qualities, and for every aviation event he organizes, he has motivated and built teams, creating an efficient work environment aimed at shared goals.

Yet, there's a cultural struggle that makes celebrating entrepreneurship challenging. Envy and resentment from those unable to grow due to their own lack of motivation, laziness, or even ideology often create stigmas, social prejudices, or concrete actions intended to induce failure in these entrepreneurs.

Sometimes, these negative individuals hold some level of power through a position in state administration, and they don't hesitate to use it through regulation or bureaucracy, adding considerable difficulties.

Queque had experienced an incident a few days prior. While flying along the coast, a mechanical issue involving a loose propeller seal forced him to make an emergency landing on a beach.

On top of the difficulty of extracting the plane, transporting it to a workshop, the lost income from the inactivity of his primary work tool, and the economic effort required for repairs, conspiratorial comments began to surface on social media from ignorant and ill-intentioned people, an unexpected but common occurrence. The need for attention, speculation in the absence of information, easy internet access, and a part of society always ready to interpret life as if it were a soap opera create favorable spaces for these groups. Worse yet, some sensationalist media and even officials are receptive to this information and act accordingly.

While we were in Trevelin, preparing the Cessna 180 to transfer it to Lobos, we noticed typical signs, especially in Queque, of someone burdened by stress from these pressures and overactivity. The light-hearted mood of summer—during the STOL takeoff and landing competition, visits from friends, and the great champion Bob Breeden—had given way to evident worry and nervousness.

It's essential as pilots to be aware of emotional indicators such as anxiety, nervousness, or worry, lower frustration tolerance, and an overwhelming feeling where demands begin to exceed capabilities before taking flight.

In the cognitive domain, pre-flight stress can cause difficulty concentrating, problems maintaining focus on tasks, and memory issues, with frequent forgetfulness and difficulty recalling details. Clouded judgment, with challenges in decision-making, is another common sign.

For a pilot, preparing for mountain flying in optimal condition goes beyond the technical skill to operate an aircraft. It requires a combination of good physical condition and a balanced mental state ready to handle adverse situations. A physically fit pilot will be better able to withstand the demands of high-altitude flights and changing weather conditions. Moreover, a stable mental state will enable quick, precise decision-making, always keeping safety as the top priority.

Knowledge of the Terrain

With the plane leveled at 6,000 feet, we had enough altitude to cross from Trevelin to Cholila through the vast Percey River valley, across the Rivadavia Range and Los Alerces National Park. After that, the terrain would descend, and we'd pass over the Carrileufu River and Lake Cholila. Those 6,000 feet were also sufficient to clear Cerro Plataforma before reaching our destination. It wasn't a direct route by any means, but there was no sense in climbing to 10,000 feet to surpass all the elevations. For this relatively short flight, it was better to follow the valleys and lakes.

As we advanced, showing off a bit of my knowledge, I pointed out to Pablo all the lakes, lagoons, and their names, as well as some of the mountains. I prided myself on knowing practically all the bodies of water, rivers, and streams from San Martín de los Andes to southern Chubut. Not only had I flown extensively in these areas, but for 30 years, my wife and I had dedicated ourselves to managing sport fishing and overseeing rivers and lakes in Chubut, Río Negro, and the national parks. I enjoyed having a large map without names and recognizing the lakes by their shapes, the rivers connecting them, and the streams feeding into them.

However, to my dismay, I realized I couldn't remember the names of many of them. How was that possible? We flew past a small lagoon on our right, and I had completely forgotten its name. We had studied it in detail once, catching Patagonian silverside that weighed nearly a kilogram, which had greatly intrigued us. To get there, we had gotten stuck with the Ford F100 from the hatchery where we worked, and it had taken quite an effort to launch the boat. I also remembered that our daughter Ailín was very young then, and we used to carry her in a bassinet on all our fishing expeditions. But now, I couldn't recall the name of the lagoon. It was immensely frustrating, and when I mentioned it to Silvia, my wife, she responded with calm conviction and blunt honesty: "It's age, dear."

But even without remembering some names, everything felt familiar to me, which made me feel secure. More than once, I had flown in marginal conditions with limited visibility, yet I dared to make certain decisions with the knowledge and confidence of what lay ahead.

Mountain flying, while challenging, is also incredibly rewarding. But to truly enjoy it, risks must be minimized, as the unpredictable nature of mountain weather, wind conditions, and irregular topography can turn a pleasant flight into a dangerous situation in seconds. This is where a crucial element comes into play: knowledge of the terrain and geography.

There are many examples of pilots venturing into unknown areas and ending up in accidents or, at the very least, major scares. While technological advancements and specialized training have reduced these risks, history reminds us that knowledge of the terrain is key to safety.

Perhaps the "Tragedy of the Andes," which occurred on October 13, 1972, is one of the most striking cases. It was a devastating plane crash involving a Fairchild FH-227D of the Uruguayan Air Force. A recent film, La Sociedad de la Nieve (The Snow Society), vividly portrays the magnitude of the accident and the survivors' struggles in the high mountains.

The plane, carrying 45 people, including a rugby team and supporters, departed from Montevideo, Uruguay, bound for Santiago, Chile. The route required crossing the Andes mountain range over one of the most dangerous sections for aviation due to the mountainous terrain and its challenging weather conditions.

From the start, the flight faced critical issues. The aircraft needed to cross high mountain terrain, and the weather conditions were particularly adverse. A severe snowstorm erupted, reducing visibility to near zero and making navigation extremely difficult. Despite the crew's efforts to maintain the planned route, the poor weather rapidly deteriorated visibility.

Facing a combination of navigation errors and extremely poor weather, the crew made crucial decisions under intense pressure. The aircraft, unable to follow the intended route due to the storm and lack of visibility, deviated significantly off course. These navigation errors, combined with an inaccurate understanding of the aircraft's location, brought the plane dangerously close to the Andes, where the terrain is very high.

One of the most critical errors involved overestimating their altitude at an incorrect geographic position. Believing they had cleared the mountains, the pilots began to descend, unaware they were still above the range. This miscalculation proved fatal.

Moreover, the navigation procedures employed during the flight were inadequate. The lack of precise navigation tools and the limited technology of the time contributed to the confusion and poor decisions. Communication with air traffic controllers was also deficient. The pilots failed to clearly convey their position and flight conditions, making it harder to receive assistance.

This tragic accident highlights a series of interrelated failures, including flight planning errors, navigation in severe weather conditions, and decision-making under critical pressure. The tragedy of the Andes is a stark reminder of the inherent dangers of flying in mountainous terrain, as well as the importance of rigorous preparation and effective management of extreme situations.

Fletcher Anderson, author of Flying the Mountain, a comprehensive manual on training single-engine aircraft for mountain flying, points out that mountain flying is statistically much more dangerous than flying over flat terrain. Despite the obvious risks, many flatland pilots venture into mountainous areas without the necessary skill and knowledge, or with aircraft unsuitable for this type of flight.

Year after year, the highest number of aviation accidents in the United States occur in Alaska, Washington, Florida, Texas, and Colorado. In Alaska, in addition to the mountains, there's the added challenge of vast distances, harsh weather caused by the proximity of the Arctic and Pacific Oceans, and a lack of roads, leading to a high number of aircraft and a large percentage of the adult population being pilots who rely on aircraft for transportation. It's common to hear stories of skilled and experienced Alaskan pilots pushing safety limits because what they're transporting is important to someone. As a result, commercial insurance in Alaska is extremely costly.

The book also references a study by Susan Baker, an epidemiologist and risk management specialist, and Margaret Lamb, a charter flight pilot, instructor, and meteorology expert, who joined forces to study aviation accidents in the Aspen, Colorado, area from 1964 to 1987. In their statistical analysis of Colorado, Baker and Lamb found that, since 90% of the state's residents do not live in the mountains, most pilots do not regularly fly in them. These are flatland pilots—many trained and experienced—but they contribute significantly to the accident count as occasional visitors.

Argentina has similar geography, with the Andes Mountain range extending north to south along one edge of the country. This means that most pilots are flatland pilots and lack experience in mountain flying.

This doesn't mean mountain pilots are more skilled, but their specific experience and knowledge of the terrain contribute to greater safety. Notably, pilots with proper training and experience have fewer accidents. In this type of geography, mountain pilots are substantially safer, though most acknowledge that they benefit from highly specialized instruction and experience simply due to where they fly.

Those of us trained in places like Esquel, El Bolsón,

Bariloche, San Martín, or Junín de los Andes, Mendoza, and other Andean cities—or pilots from Chile—accept that we fly in rugged terrain and naturally adopt practices like locating potential emergency landing spots on roads, beaches, streams, or meadows, and flying with more attention to the outside than the cockpit. But flying on the plains is challenging for us.

I'm a case in point. I've spent my life flying in the mountains. Now I live in Lobos, in the province of Buenos Aires. My flying is different now, and I don't feel comfortable. I miss the visual references of lakes and mountains, replaced by an infinite, flat horizon, and I frequently get lost. The traffic unsettles me; I struggle to communicate, and airports like Morón or San Fernando intimidate me because I don't know the landmarks. I don't recognize the Matanza River or the "Rowing Canal." The towns, roads, and lagoons all look the same to me, and a field that recently served as a clear green marker suddenly vanishes when it's harvested. I find it difficult to rely so heavily on instruments and to fly in visual corridors. And every time I navigate to General Rodríguez, I'm astounded by the disorderly, intense traffic.

For that reason, my main flight now is to Fortín Lobos Air Club to have a coffee at the skydiving canteen and meet up with friends. If I need to take a longer flight, I inevitably head south, away from Baires Terminal Area.

Terrain knowledge is an invaluable tool for any pilot aspiring to fly in mountainous regions. This knowledge not only enhances safety but also boosts the pilot's confidence and competence.

In modern aviation, pilots have access to various tools and technologies to help navigate mountainous terrain. Beyond detailed topographic maps, digital systems and advanced GPS systems allow pilots to plan safe routes and avoid obstacles.

Many of these digital systems are free to use, available in web, desktop, and mobile versions, accessible on multiple devices, making them versatile for different contexts and purposes. They serve as learning tools, satisfy curiosity, or meet the real need to plan a flight, enabling route plotting and perspective-based terrain evaluation in a simulated flight.

With these applications, it's possible to view any corner of the planet with great precision, whether in two or three dimensions. One of their most impressive features is the ability to view landscapes in 3D, providing an immersive experience for virtually exploring mountainous regions.

This is complemented by information layers adding details on roads, borders, points of interest, and historical and demographic data, enriching the exploration experience.

Experienced pilots also have valuable lessons and insights to share. Their testimonies offer unique perspectives on the importance of terrain knowledge. Accident analyses also provide useful information on common errors and how to avoid them. Learning from these cases can significantly improve the preparation and safety of pilots flying in mountainous areas.

Mountain Weather

We were already directly above Lake Cholila, flying close to Cerro Puntiagudo to shorten the route toward Cerro Plataforma, the last elevated obstacle before beginning our descent to LZA. Our airstrip, the one my father had built so many years ago and that we managed to legalize after 17 years of paperwork, lay to our right. We didn't have time to land and visit the place that had been our home for a good part of our lives. We both looked at it without saying a word, but we were thinking the same thing—thoughts filled with nostalgia and memories.

I tried to clear my mind and focus on the flight. The lake was like a mirror, indicating absolute calm on the surface, making our flight very comfortable. For a while now, I had avoided flying in windy conditions, choosing the early morning hours or selecting the best days from the weather forecasts to plan my flights.

There was also no movement in the air mass at our altitude, although lenticular clouds could be seen to the east, and a formation to the west suggested a meteorological disturbance for the following day.

We tried calling Queque, but he was likely already over the Turbio River, and the mountain barriers prevented us from hearing him or him hearing us. It's typical for VHF signals to be lost among the geographical obstacles unless there's a bounce. Controllers are aware of this, and when they clear a flight in Bariloche or Esquel, they take into account that even within the control area, the radial signal is lost almost immediately.

Although I was well-trained in reading the mountain and predicting where updrafts or downdrafts would come from or which slope I should follow, the turbulence generated is always uncomfortable. It strains the aircraft structure, and since most of my flights are cargo flights, it requires securely tying down what I'm transporting. Additionally, flying from Cholila to LZA with a westerly wind means dealing with a downdraft until crossing Cerro Plataforma, with significant turbulence at the confluence of two valleys—Blanco Creek valley and the Tigre River valley. Many times, I found myself spiraling up on the southern side of the lake to reach a safe altitude, even with the altitude loss from the downdrafts, to safely cross from the Cholila valley to the Turbio

River valley and Lake Puelo.

The return trip was different. The prevailing westerly wind traveling along the long Turbio River valley collided with Cerro Derrumbe, creating an updraft. Part of the wind also hit Cerro Plataforma, causing the same effect. Once we crossed it, we no longer worried about downdrafts, some of which could reach 2,000 feet per minute. But after crossing, we would encounter the friendly Lake Cholila. Once over it, the wind was more laminar and unidirectional from west to east, aligned with the runway.

Pilots need to be trained to interpret the visual cues of these conditions. In the field, this is called "reading the mountain" and adjusting the flight to avoid dangerous areas, identifying where downdrafts, rotors, and updrafts are, and knowing which side of the mountain to follow for lift. Meteorological knowledge is useful not only for pre-flight planning but also for real-time decision-making. Mountainous geography generates specific atmospheric phenomena that can surprise even the most experienced pilot if they aren't prepared for them. It's crucial to analyze the various facets of meteorology in the context of mountain flight, such as the effect of topography on moving air masses.

An informed pilot can continually assess weather conditions during the flight, adjusting course and altitude to avoid bad weather or severe turbulence. The ability to make quick and accurate decisions in response to changing environmental conditions is valuable in mountain flying.

Early identification of signs of deteriorating weather, such as the appearance of vertically developing clouds or reduced visibility, also allows for preventive measures to avoid dangerous situations. The ability to divert, change altitude, or even abort the flight if conditions become unsafe are options that should be anticipated.

Elevations act as natural barriers that alter air flow, creating complex and variable weather patterns. When wind encounters a mountain, it's forced to rise, leading to cloud formation and precipitation on the windward slopes. This is what happens with moist winds from the Pacific that collide with the Andes. Additionally, this upward air movement can generate strong updrafts, known as orographic wind, which can be used to gain altitude in challenging situations.

Orographic wind is used by gliders in a condition known as "dynamic flight." Unlike "thermal flight," where lift is produced by warmer convective currents rising, in this case, it uses the push of the wind, which is much more predictable and easier to locate.

In San Carlos de Bariloche, east of Lake Nahuel Huapi, stands Cerro Villegas, about 750 meters above ground level, which receives a continuous, steady northwesterly wind, lifting it like a ramp and creating a dynamic condition widely used by glider pilots.

The tow plane carries the gliders from nearby runways and releases them at 600 meters near the hill. The gliders then join the updraft and can stay there indefinitely as long as there's wind or climb well above the summit, giving them a wider flight area. It's a great attraction not only for glider pilots but also for tourists who book these flights as sightseeing excursions. Often, these flights are accompanied by condors and other birds of prey, which take advantage of the same dynamic lift, sharing the airspace without disturbance.

However, these same currents can be dangerous for single-engine aircraft, as the air flowing and spilling down the leeward side of the ridge and moving downhill becomes turbulent, forming whirlwinds that can create severe turbulence and sudden changes in airspeed.

In areas with mountain intersections, where valleys guide the wind in different directions due to irregular terrain, "mechanical turbulence" occurs. This happens when wind collides with these obstacles, creating vortices and disturbances in the air. Mechanical turbulence is more intense near the ground and around peaks and ridges. For small aircraft pilots, mechanical turbulence poses a significant risk, as it can cause abrupt changes in altitude and aircraft attitude, making control difficult.

A particularly important phenomenon resulting from the interaction between wind and mountains is mountain waves. These oscillations in the airflow can extend to heights far above the mountains themselves and be extremely stable and regular, giving pilots the opportunity to reach high altitudes.

In many cases, microclimates form, differing drastically from the general forecast. A valley might be shrouded in dense fog, while a nearby peak remains clear. Understanding this variability is essential, as visibility and flight conditions can change within minutes. Pilots must be able to interpret and anticipate these changes to adjust their routes and altitudes accordingly.

Fog is another common meteorological phenomenon in mountainous regions, especially in valleys and basins. It occurs when air near the ground cools enough for water vapor to condense into tiny, suspended water droplets, forming a cloud at ground level. Fog can drastically reduce visibility, complicating takeoffs, landings, and in-flight navigation. Pilots must be alert to conditions that favor fog formation, such as clear, windless nights.

Temperature inversions are also critical for pilots flying in mountainous areas. A temperature inversion occurs when a layer

The rotor forms at the base of the waves, where the air rapidly descends from the crest and interacts with the lower layers of the atmosphere. This downward flow collides with the Earth's surface or slower-moving air layers, creating intense turbulence characterized by sharply defined updrafts and downdrafts, as well as irregular horizontal movements.

of warm air sits abnormally over a layer of cooler air, inhibiting convection and air mixing. This can trap pollutants and moisture near the ground, creating foggy conditions or trapping smoke in valleys. Temperature inversions can reduce visibility and affect air quality, adding another complication.

The ability to interpret weather maps is important for planning mountain flights. Atmospheric pressure maps, for example, can reveal high and low-pressure systems influencing weather conditions. Upper-level wind maps provide information on wind direction and speed, helping pilots anticipate turbulence zones and mountain waves. Additionally, cloud and precipitation maps allow pilots to assess the risk of bad weather along their planned route.

To navigate safely in the complex mountain environment, single-engine pilots must use various tools and resources to interpret weather changes. These include aviation weather reports, short- and long-term forecasts, satellite images, and weather radars. Modern technology provides pilots with unprecedented access to real-time weather information, enabling more informed and safer decisions.

Aviation weather reports, known as METAR and TAF, are vital sources of information for pilots. METAR provides current weather observations, including temperature, pressure, visibility, cloud cover, and wind conditions at specific airports. TAF, on the other hand, offers short-term forecasts covering up to 24 hours, providing information on possible changes in weather conditions. When available, it's advisable to review these reports before the flight and stay updated on any changes.

Satellite images and weather radar are powerful tools for real-time weather monitoring. Satellite images provide a global view of weather conditions, showing the location and movement of clouds and storms. Weather radar detects precipitation and can reveal storm intensity and movement. These tools allow pilots to identify bad weather areas and adjust their routes accordingly.

Meteorology apps and software have revolutionized how pilots access and use weather information. These tools offer detailed forecasts, interactive maps, and real-time alerts on adverse weather conditions. Some apps also provide flight simulations based on weather data, allowing pilots to practice decision-making in different weather scenarios. Using these tools can greatly enhance the safety and efficiency of mountain flights.

The ability to interpret and anticipate atmospheric conditions is crucial for flight safety and efficiency. The typical weather phenomena in mountainous regions can sometimes quickly exceed an unprepared pilot crew's response capacity. Therefore, studying and understanding meteorology are not optional but fundamental for any pilot venturing into mountain skies.

This knowledge translates into a greater ability to make informed decisions, adapt to changing conditions, and ultimately ensure the safety of the aircraft and its occupants. Meteorology thus becomes a vital tool in the arsenal of any mountain pilot, enabling safer and more successful flights in some of the most challenging terrains on the planet. A deep understanding of mountain meteorology is, therefore, not only a skill but a fundamental necessity for any pilot aspiring to fly safely and successfully in these complex environments.

Training and Knowledge of Aircraft Performance

Cerro Plataforma was behind us. In front of us lay the familiar sight of Lake Puelo, and beyond it, the towns of Lago

Puelo and El Bolsón, shrouded in a faint blue haze, the result of the smoke from hundreds of wood stoves—the primary heating source in these areas.

To our left, the Turbio River unfolded, stretching along a very long valley that branches into four smaller canyons at the upper end, each with its own rivers that converge almost at the same point, forming the main channel. The river originates in the mountains far to the west, near the border with Chile, then turns northward, flowing into Lake Puelo, and eventually discharges westward again toward the Pacific Ocean. It's a very unique watershed.

Moreover, on the Argentine side, the lake lies at 190 meters above sea level, making it one of the lowest passes to cross the mountain range.

We continued our descent, merging into the Lake Esperanza sub-basin. To enter, we had to navigate through a narrow and deep valley. Below us ran the Bravo or Esperanza River, with stretches of strong rapids and a large waterfall that, over time, had formed an impressive pool. It's very hard to reach by land due to the steep terrain.

The entry approach heads west, and depending on altitude, all you can see ahead is a wall. Following the river's course toward its source, it turns 90 degrees south, where another slope looms ahead, but after a short distance, the valley opens westward again, and suddenly the airstrip appears, with Lake Esperanza behind it.

The initial approach many times, we began configurating the aircraft, preparing it for a short final as soon as the runway came into view. Flying slowly with a notch of flaps, we zigzagged over the river before making a final right turn where the runway appeared. Fortunately, there was a snow-free area on the southern edge, more exposed to the sun, which would have allowed us to land without much trouble. However, we didn't see Queque's PA-18 at the end of the runway.

While on final, we attempted communication again, and this time, he responded. He informed us he was flying on the other side of the lake, near the Western Outpost—the cabin at the far end, accessible only by an equestrian trail or boat across the lake.

What was he doing there? He told us over the radio that he had a plan: to land wherever he could, as the boat for crossing was unavailable. In response, we aborted our landing, retracted the flaps, applied power, climbed again, and crossed to the other side of the lake ourselves. We asked him to wait. I had previously evaluated a likely landing spot several times without actually landing, but I had measured it, cleared some logs, and studied the surface. I wanted to show him where to land.

We had good communication, and the spot he had already chosen was the same one I would have suggested, so we kept orbiting while he prepared for the maneuver.

After carefully examining the area and making several passes, we realized he had already made his decision. The small plane began to slow down, giving the impression of moving in slow motion. He made a gentle turn, clearing a few trees, and then, with a delicate glide, touched his "bush wheels" down on the improvised landing strip.

From our vantage point, we watched as, in an impeccable maneuver, the Piper PA-18 rolled a few meters, stopped, then pivoted its nose 180 degrees and taxied toward the cabin. It was an eloquent demonstration of this pilot's skill and training, his deep knowledge of his aircraft's performance, and a reaffirmation of the concepts he had long advocated regarding the importance of seriously considering "Bush Flying" as a segment of general aviation that should be promoted and supported.

Bush flying is a specialized branch of general aviation that focuses on operating aircraft in remote and often inaccessible areas. This style of flying, which often involves light aircraft with a great capacity for short takeoff and landing (STOL), is characterized by its adaptability to challenging terrain, adverse weather conditions, and improvised airstrips. The importance of bush flying goes beyond the simple pleasure of flying. Its applicability in rescue missions, evacuations, food and medicine transport makes it a crucial component for the safety and well-being of remote and isolated communities.

In the winter of 2020, the entire Cushamen area, a town in Chubut province, faced a massive snowfall that left many residents stranded. This snowstorm was particularly intense and had a significant impact on the region, which is already known for its extreme winter conditions.

The snow accumulation not only blocked roads and main routes but also caused the death of a large number of livestock. Conditions were so harsh that residents were forced to shelter inside their homes with their most valuable or cherished animals, even burning their corrals and fences for heating. This situation highlighted the vulnerability of remote communities to extreme weather events and the importance of having contingency plans and efficient response systems to address such emergencies.

With Queque's Cessna 172 XP and our Cessna 180, we volunteered to provide aerial assistance. We knew an army helicopter was delivering food, but the stranded residents also needed supplies for their animals and batteries for their radios.

Knowing we could drop bags with these supplies, we made ourselves available.

We also knew that, given the scale of the need, our help might be limited, so we invited several colleagues to participate. Immediately, around twenty planes from various parts of the country volunteered to join this solidarity mission.

Despite the climate emergency putting many lives and animals at risk, and the fact that we were covering the costs of the flights and supplies ourselves, the government blocked this assistance, preventing any of those planes from carrying out this mission by imposing regulations and administrative procedures incomprehensible in such circumstances.

The situation underscored deficiencies in emergency coordination and quick response, especially during a pandemic, when additional restrictions further complicated logistics. Government bureaucracy proved a significant obstacle to effective crisis assistance, and the lack of flexibility in procedures contributed to the difficulty of adequately addressing the emergency in Cushamen.

Finally, only I was authorized to perform the overflights with the Cessna 180, leaving Queque's XP grounded. I still had to go through the arduous process of requesting an exemption, classified as "Support Flight for Chubut Civil Defense to Assist Residents Isolated by Snow."

So, both of us, frustrated, set out in the Cessna 180 to help as much as we could, knowing that our contribution would be modest. We left the XP in Cholila and headed toward El Maitén, the nearest airstrip to Cushamen. A wealthy friend, concerned about the situation, offered support, and we purchased a substantial amount of feed bags and grain. With the help of airstrip chief

Hernán Cerieldín and friends from the aeroclub, we repacked them into smaller, stronger 10 kg bags, allowing us to drop them from the windows. We painted them red tobe able tobe seen in the snow and departed with the plane at its maximum takeoff weight.

The scene was bleak. The houses were barely visible, but the tall poplars indicated their locations. To our left, and quite far away, we could see the road, partially cleared, which we noted as a potential emergency landing spot.

We located the first homestead, flew over it, and immediately saw several people come out, signaling to us. We quickly assessed the maneuver we needed to perform. We first determined the best spot to drop the bags, as close as possible to where the people were standing. Since the location was on a hillside with several gullies, we had to begin our descent from the highest point to ensure that when we pulled up, the terrain wouldn't take us by surprise. The pass had to be as low and slow as possible to ensure the bags would land where we intended, while also minimizing the risk of them hitting the stabilizer. The weight of the bags and low speed would help prevent this.

Once the maneuver was defined, Queque slid his seat back, placed three 10-kilogram bags on his knees, and opened the window. I set a notch of flaps to slow us down, aligned the plane with a fence, and dodged the poplars for a low pass.

Queque released the bags in quick succession. As soon as they were out, I made a climbing left turn, allowing us to see people running toward them. We made a second, slightly higher pass, and were pleased to see them lifting the bags and signaling they had received them.

We repeated this operation several times at each

homestead, searching for a group of poplars and heading in that direction. In almost every case, we received the same response.

However, at some places, no one came out. We saw tracks around the houses but no signs of life. Clearly, they were there, but for some reason, they weren't showing any signs of life. We feared the worst, and a deep sadness overcame us. This was confirmed once the contingency ended, and rescue teams arrived at those places. There had been human casualties, in addition to the massive animal losses.

We imagined that, if we had skis, we might have been able to do more, perhaps even perform some rescues. The steppe offers many flat areas, further smoothed by the snow. However, given the challenges in obtaining authorization for overflights, it was unimaginable to think we'd be allowed to land on the snow, even with the proper aircraft.

We were far from what Donald "Don" Edward Sheldon had inspired—a pioneer of "Bush Flying" and a renowned rescuer in Alaska's most inhospitable regions. His skill in flying under extreme conditions, combined with his bravery and dedication, made him a legendary figure in aviation history.

Don Sheldon was one of the most iconic and respected mountain pilots in Alaska. Born on November 21, 1921, in Michigan, USA, he joined the Air Force as a young man, serving as a turret gunner and mechanic on B-17 bombers during World War II. After the war, he moved to Alaska, where he discovered his true calling in mountain aviation. He bought a single-engine Cessna 180, and over the years, he became an expert in landing on unstable surfaces like glaciers and deep snow. He modified his Cessna 180 and a Piper Super Cub with retractable skis, enabling him to make the first snow landings on Ruth Glacier at Mount

McKinley (Denali), North America's highest peak, and throughout the Alaska Range from 1947 until his passing in 1975.

Though most of his flights involved transporting supplies, equipment, and people, he also conducted numerous rescues of stranded climbers, hikers in distress, lost hunters, or survivors of crashes.

From then on, bush flying in Alaska became not only a respected activity but essential for many communities, deeply intertwined with daily life and economic development in this vast, remote region. The extreme climate and limited ground transportation infrastructure have positioned bush pilots and their specially adapted aircraft as essential.

One of the most notable aspects of bush flying in Alaska is access to remote areas. Many parts of the state are unreachable by road, and in winter, ground transport becomes even more challenging due to harsh weather conditions. Bush planes keep these areas connected, facilitating access, delivering food, shelter, and medicine. Scientific exploration and environmental research on wildlife and climate change also heavily rely on this type of aviation.

Even adventure tourism, as well as sport fishing and hunting in Alaska, depend largely on bush planes. These aircraft transport fishers and hunters to otherwise inaccessible places, supporting a vital source of income for the region.

Beyond these essential functions, bush flying is a core part of Alaska's local economy. It provides jobs for pilots, mechanics, and other aviation professionals and supports local businesses dependent on air transport.

However, Alaska isn't unique in this regard. Similar stories

abound worldwide, such as that of Tom Curtis, an Australian bush pilot who rescued a group of tourists stranded in the Simpson Desert. His lightweight aircraft, capable of landing on sandy terrain, transported the tourists to a hospital due to dehydration and sun exposure.

In the Amazon rainforest, Syd Bell, known for his knowledge of the region, located and rescued a family of tourists lost during a jungle expedition. He landed in an improvised clearing and brought them to safety.

In the Himalayas, Maurizio Folini in Nepal conducted an emergency rescue of climbers affected by altitude sickness. Using a STOL aircraft, he landed on an improvised high-altitude strip and evacuated the climbers to a hospital in Kathmandu.

Johnny May, a Canadian Arctic bush pilot, rescued a team of scientists isolated by breaking sea ice. Flying a ski-equipped aircraft, he landed on a small, stable ice strip and evacuated the scientists before the ice completely fractured.

These examples highlight the importance of this category within general aviation. In any emergency, speed and precision are critical for saving lives, and these planes, equipped with large wheels, powerful engines, and STOL capabilities, can land and take off on makeshift, short, and unprepared strips—such as riverbanks, beaches, and forest clearings—to save lives.

The primary aircraft used in bush flying are the Piper Super Cub PA-18 and the Cessna 180 or Cessna 185. They can be adapted for extremely short takeoffs and landings, allowing operation on improvised strips, or fitted with floats for lake landings and skis for snow landings.

However, besides having an aircraft adapted for such

restrictive conditions, pilots must be well-trained and deeply understand their aircraft's performance in terms of maneuverability and limitations.

Density Altitude

Single-engine aircraft have specific limitations that must be understood and respected, such as the relationship between altitude and engine performance. As altitude increases, air density decreases, reducing engine power and affecting the aircraft's climb capability. Pilots must be well-informed about their aircraft's power curves and know how to adjust their flight to maintain safe performance. This includes managing the fuel-air mixture to optimize engine efficiency or prevent power loss.

In Patagonia, the average height of mountains is around 2,000 meters above sea level, with notable exceptions such as Cerro Tronador and Lanín Volcano, which stand out in the mountain range. There are others, like Cerro Tres Picos and Dos Picos, that slightly exceed this height, but in all cases, to safely fly over most summits and avoid being affected by orographic turbulence, one must fly well above them—at flight level 90 or higher. In regions further north, like Mendoza to Salta, much higher levels are required.

Therefore, when forced to fly at higher altitudes for navigation between two relatively distant points, such as from Esquel to Bariloche or Chapelco, some considerations must be kept in mind. One of these is Density Altitude, an essential concept in aviation, which refers to air density expressed in terms of the altitude at which this density would be found in the standard atmosphere. This altitude is influenced by factors such as temperature, barometric pressure, and humidity. When temperature is high, air density decreases, raising the density altitude. Similarly, lower barometric pressure or increased humidity also reduces air density.

Aircraft performance is significantly affected by this density altitude. Engines, relying on oxygen in the air for combustion, experience reduced efficiency and power as density altitude increases. Likewise, wings generate less lift due to lower air density, meaning takeoff and landing speeds must be higher at elevated airstrips. Additionally, propellers lose efficiency under these conditions, reducing available thrust. On the other hand, this "lighter" air, with more widely spaced molecules, creates less drag, translating to higher true airspeed and consequent fuel savings.

It's important to remember that the amount of oxygen used by engines as an oxidizer decreases in the air as the aircraft moves away from the surface. To maintain combustion efficiency, the so-called stoichiometric mixture must be managed through the appropriate control. This refers to the ideal proportion of oxygen and fuel for complete combustion. The reference value for this mixture is 14.7 kilograms of air per kilogram of fuel. Proper mixture management prevents any of these components from being released in excess.

A stoichiometric mixture maximizes engine efficiency and minimizes pollutant emissions. However, in practice, engines do not always operate exactly at these conditions. In some cases, such as during rapid acceleration or when seeking maximum power, it may be necessary to enrich the mixture (add more fuel) or lean it out (reduce the amount of fuel) to achieve the desired performance. Adjusting the air-fuel mixture in piston engines ensures efficient performance at different density altitudes.

At lower altitudes, where air density is greater, a richer fuel mixture is required. This means adding more fuel relative to the air, as there is enough oxygen to support efficient combustion.

However, as the aircraft ascends and the available oxygen decreases, it becomes necessary to lean the mixture, reducing the fuel relative to the air. Maintaining an overly rich mixture at higher altitudes can lead to incomplete combustion, which not only reduces engine power but also increases fuel consumption and can cause performance issues.

To adjust the mixture, pilots typically use several methods. The most common one is indicated by the aircraft's operations manual, using the Exhaust Gas Temperature (EGT) gauge. According to the manual, by adjusting the mixture to reach maximum exhaust gas temperature and then enriching it slightly by about 50°F (50°F ROP), efficient combustion is ensured while preventing engine overheating. In some aircraft, a fuel flow sensor is also used to adjust the mixture optimally, based on the amount of fuel flowing to the engine. Additionally, experienced pilots may adjust the mixture based on the sound and smoothness of the engine's operation, seeking a smooth and trouble-free run.

During different stages of flight, mixture adjustment also varies. At takeoff, the mixture is usually richer to provide maximum power. However, as the aircraft ascends, the pilot should progressively lean the mixture. During cruise, the mixture is adjusted to maximize fuel efficiency, which generally involves further leaning. Finally, during descent and landing, the mixture may need to be enriched again as air density increases, ensuring the engine doesn't stall as power is reduced. Incorrect mixture adjustment can lead to issues such as overheating, power loss, and other problems that could compromise safety.

This type of mixture operation, indicated by the manuals, is called ROP, meaning "Rich of Peak." In this context, "rich" refers to a mixture with more fuel relative to the air, and "peak" refers to the point where exhaust gas temperature (EGT) is highest.

When an engine is operated ROP, the air-fuel mixture is adjusted to be slightly richer than the point at which maximum exhaust gas temperature is reached. This technique has traditionally been considered safe because a richer mixture tends to cool the engine, reducing the risk of overheating and detonation, albeit at the cost of higher fuel consumption.

The approach outlined in these manuals suggests operating with a richer mixture to maximize power and reduce overheating risks. In fact, most older pilots fly this way, especially in mountain flying, where power is a significant factor in flight operation.

However, on longer flights, the technique of flying with a lean mixture, or "Lean of Peak" (LOP), has begun to be used, thanks to new engine monitoring technologies. This technique improves fuel efficiency and reduces wear. In a LOP mixture setting, the engine runs with a lower proportion of fuel relative to the air, compared to the "Rich of Peak" (ROP) setting, where a richer fuel mixture is used.

LOP flying is mainly employed during cruising, when power demand is steady, and a stable mixture setting can be maintained without compromising engine operation. It is recommended when cruise altitude allows good airflow in the engine and stable cooling conditions, when maximum engine power isn't required, and when instrumentation is available to carefully monitor cylinder and exhaust gas temperatures.

The fourth section of this book provides a more detailed description of this technique.

Effects of Altitude on the Pilot

Not only is the aircraft affected by altitude, but pilots are as well. Flying at high altitudes can impact crew members in various ways due to the reduction in atmospheric pressure and decreased oxygen availability. As altitude increases, the decrease in available oxygen can lead to hypoxia, a condition in which the blood does not receive enough oxygen.

One of my father's anecdotes, which he always shared at gatherings with his comrades, centered on a high-altitude photographic flight conducted in the mountainous area between Mendoza and Neuquén. At the time, he was a young mechanic who had taken on significant responsibility as the caretaker of the Avro Lincoln B016 aircraft, the same one displayed today at the entrance to the Air Force base in Villa Reynolds.

As the mechanic, he had taken a great deal of time meticulously checking everything, but he felt an uncomfortable tingling that comes with the sense that something might have been overlooked. However, the aircraft—a true flying fortress—was already taxiing toward the runway with all four engines running. He reviewed his checklist repeatedly until he realized what he was missing: his oxygen mask. That small piece of equipment was absolutely necessary to avoid ending up unconscious like a rag doll at several thousand meters' altitude.

But without hesitation, he took the course that only a reckless young man would choose. He decided not to say anything, thus avoiding reprimand from the commander and a potential decision to delay or postpone the flight. Yet, the greatest fear was facing the embarrassing situation of the entire crew seeing him as the rookie who forgot the basics. In those early flying days, the fear of reprimand was insignificant compared to the dread of being ridiculed.

What he remembers from that situation is hearing the pilot's voice over the intercom, saying they were concluding the mission, descending through 3,000 meters, and could remove their masks. As he regained consciousness, he realized he had been unconscious for the entire flight and was now hanging from his harness.

A more serious incident involved a Swiss pilot who visited us in Cholila. He had crossed the Atlantic solo in a small two-seater Dynamic. He liked flying high to avoid storms, but while flying in Latin America, he struggled to refill his oxygen equipment or replenish his oxygen bottles, essential for high-altitude flying. He was en route to the United States when hypoxia overcame him, resulting in a crash against Cotopaxi Volcano in Ecuador.

Hypoxia symptoms include dizziness, fatigue, headache, confusion, and, in severe cases, even loss of consciousness. Additionally, pressure changes can cause barotrauma, affecting the body's air-filled cavities, such as the ears, sinuses, and lungs, leading to pain or physical damage.

Altitude can also impact a pilot's perception and balance, leading to spatial disorientation, a dangerous situation that can make controlling the aircraft more difficult. Vision may also be affected, potentially reducing visual acuity and color distinction.

Another common effect is decreased cognitive performance. Lack of oxygen can hinder concentration, slow reaction times, and impair decision-making. Additionally, the dry air in pressurized cabins can lead to dehydration if pilots don't consume enough water.

Finally, at extremely high altitudes, some may experience altitude sickness, with symptoms like nausea, vomiting, fatigue, and headache. To mitigate these effects, pilots receive training in flight physiology and use oxygen equipment and pressurization systems in aircraft suitable for those altitudes. It's essential that they stay well-hydrated and rested to maintain alertness and

LV-FZG

performance.

Training a pilot for mountainous flight is not merely an extension of general flight instruction; it is a discipline that takes on specialized aspects, addressing the risks and complexities inherent to these environments.

The combination of specialized training, deep knowledge of the aircraft's performance, and adequate psychological preparation are essential for safely and effectively flying single-engine planes in mountainous areas. The ability to interpret weather conditions, execute specific maneuvers, and meticulously plan each flight ensures that pilots can face the risks associated with this type of flying. This comprehensive approach not only enhances safety but also contributes to increasing the pilot's skill and professionalism, raising operational standards in general aviation.

Mountain Flying Techniques

It was 1992. A group of pilots from the Bariloche Aeroclub was flying with instructor Gabriel Gurlekian, who was preparing us to pass the exam for Controlled VFR certification. At that time, this was a stage that came after the private pilot course, and a directive had been issued stating that anyone without this qualification on their license would not be permitted to operate in controlled airports. We wouldn't even be able to access the Bariloche airport, even though the aeroclub was within the CTR control zone.

Several of us were aiming for this new license. The aeroclub only had an Aero Boero 115 and two ultralight Flightstar planes, one single-seater and the other a two-seater. None were sufficiently equipped to be used for this course, much less for taking the exam. Therefore, the El Maitén aeroclub lent us its Piper Cherokee 140, LV-DHP, and the Esquel aeroclub provided a Piper Archer II, LV-ARO, both from Chincul and very well equipped.

The inspector, Mr. Juan Carlos Sánchez, was scheduled to come the following day, and Gabriel was making last-minute adjustments and evaluating if we were well-prepared for the exam. He was an excellent instructor, with a good teaching approach, and his lessons were well received.

Suddenly, we heard the wail of an ambulance siren approaching the aeroclub. We hadn't registered any accidents, but hearing that sound was always worrisome. A man in a white coat, whom we inferred was a doctor, got out and requested an urgent flight to El Bolsón. A girl had been injured when a ladder fell on her, and she needed to be transferred to Bariloche urgently. Back then, the road was unpaved and very challenging, so the best option was to fly her, if an aircraft was available.

Being a member of the Esquel Aeroclub, with over 15 years of experience and around 600 flight hours, Gabriel asked me to undertake the flight in the Archer. It was fueled, and as a pilot eager to fly, I was always ready. I would fly alone because I also had to bring the girl's father, and she might need to lie down, so we had a small stretcher available. The ambulance would be waiting at the aeroclub.

The weather was not ideal, but it allowed me to reach El Bolsón without issue. The girl didn't seem to be in a severe condition since she got into the plane with minimal assistance. Her father settled into the front seat, and we quickly departed for Bariloche.

But it had started to rain. Visibility was still good, and it was clear to the north, giving me confidence as I had come through the same valley on my flight to El Bolsón.

However, conditions change rapidly. As we progressed, I noticed the passage just before Lake Guillelmo was closing up. The terrain rises in what is known as the "Pampa del Toro," at the end of the

"Cañadón de la Mosca," with clouds touching the ground. Given the situation, I looked for an alternate route, which involves flying low over the Villegas River until reaching the "Las Mellizas" lagoons, the highest point located at the Atlantic-Pacific watershed, then descending along the Pichileufu River. If the cloud cover allows, the goal is to connect with the Ñirihuau River, which leads directly to runway 29 at Bariloche.

I reached the Villegas valley, but it was closed off too. I turned back and saw that access to El Bolsón was still possible despite the rain, which was light enough to maintain sufficient visibility. Above me, there was a beautiful blue sky with a large opening in the clouds that allowed for a spiral climb. If things got complicated, I had the option to return to El Bolsón, having failed my medical mission.

I applied more thrus and began climbing in a steady turn with the nose up over this large valley, using the Bailey bridge over the Villegas River and the Gendarmería Nacional checkpoint as reference points. I kept myself vertical to that point, and I loved that plane. It responded wonderfully. We climbed above the cloud layer and set a course for Bariloche, flying over the mountain peaks with the great Cerro Tronador to my left, serving as a visual reference.

In Bariloche, the clouds were breaking up, allowing me descendend without any issues, land, and hand over the patient to the doctor waiting at the aeroclub.

I have fond memories of Gabriel Gurlekian, not only because he was an excellent instructor but also a kind and generous person. I was deeply saddened by his passing. Not long after this incident, he suffered an accident in Córdoba in an ultralight Falcon XP due to the detachment of one of the wings, resulting in a violent crash to the ground.

The Civil Aviation Accident Investigation Board later determined that a fracture occurred in the left wing's strut mount to the fuselage, originating from material fatigue and a manufacturing defect. Other contributing factors included deficient maintenance and a fuel tank with a higher capacity than allowed, adding additional weight.

Returning to mountain flying, I recount this situation to introduce the topic of mountain flying techniques across the Andes and its foothills.

Flying in Valleys and Canyons

Typically, since most flights are relatively short, routes often follow valleys and avoid high elevations. However, safe flying in valleys and canyons requires terrain knowledge, constant weather monitoring, and practice in executing precise maneuvers under pressure.

Mountain valleys aren't linear routes, so flights are indirect and may include tight turns, abrupt climb, and areas where the wind changes direction unpredictably. For safe flying, the technique begins with a visual and cartographic survey of the area, identifying valley entry and exit points and determining an altitude high enough to clear any elevated terrain that may suddenly appear.

Often, pilots must fly over very narrow valleys. In these cases, it's recommended to fly along one side of the valley, maintaining a safe distance but staying close to one side of the slope. This allows for a quicker and wider turn if a return becomes necessary. It's best to fly near the windward side—the side where the wind hits the mountains. This positioning offers the advantage of using the updrafts created as the wind rises along the slope, providing a "cushion" of air that can be vital for maintaining or gaining altitude if needed. Additionally, flying on this side helps avoid turbulence and downdrafts that often form on the leeward side, which can be especially dangerous in confined spaces. It's also recommended to fly downstream in such valleys, where the terrain descends, and the valley usually widens.

When a pilot enters a narrow valley, the margin for maneuvering is significantly reduced, and decisions must be made precisely and quickly. The first rule is to understand that in a narrow valley, escape routes are limited; therefore, maintaining a clear exit path is essential in case conditions change suddenly or the flight becomes unsustainable.

Choosing the right altitude is another critical aspect. Flying too low in a narrow valley limits options for turns or emergency maneuvers and increases the risk of encountering unexpected obstacles like trees, rocks, snow, or other terrain features.

Flying in narrow valleys also requires careful speed management. Flying too fast can reduce reaction time when facing an obstacle or a sudden change in the valley's direction, while flying too slow can lead to a loss of lift, especially in tight turns where the plane's bank angle is steep. The speed must be high enough to maintain firm control of the plane but low enough to allow for safe, effective maneuvers in the limited valley space. Often, it's helpful to use a notch of flaps to maintain good lift while staying within the white arc on the airspeed indicator.

Visibility is another factor to consider. In a narrow valley, visibility may be limited by sharp turns, as in the entry to the Del Turco creek valley from the north toward Cholila, or reduced by the terrain's relief or weather conditions like low clouds or fog. For this reason, it's essential for the pilot to remain vigilant and be prepared to adapt quickly to changes in the visual environment. The pilot must be alert and anticipate what might lie beyond each curve in the valley, planning escape routes or altitude changes in advance.

Decision-making is critical in this environment. If the valley begins to close or conditions become unfavorable, the pilot must be willing to abort the mission and turn back before the situation becomes irreversible. The ability to make quick and firm decisions can make the difference between a safe flight and an emergency situation.

Familiarity with the terrain is an advantage for local pilots. Familiarity with the region and local experience shouldn't be underestimated. Each mountain range has its peculiarities, and pilots with experience in a specific area are better able to recognize terrain cues and meteorological phenomena that may not be obvious to less experienced pilots. This knowledge cannot be replaced by any technical skill; it is the result of accumulated experience and constant observation. However, it can be shared: any visiting pilot, even one with considerable experience, should seek advice from local pilots before setting out and, if possible, fly accompanied, even in another aircraft, with constant communication—better yet.

Flying in narrow valleys is an operation that combines technique, judgment, and a deep respect for the environment, where every movement must be calculated and executed precisely. With proper preparation and a cautious mindset, it's possible to navigate these valleys safely.

It may happen that the valley closes in, that we don't have enough altitude to reach the next valley where the slope starts to descend, or that sudden cloud cover obstructs visibility, forcing a 180-degree turn to reverse course. In any of these scenarios, we must act quickly and decisively but without panic, carefully assessing the best way to proceed.

First, consider altitude relative to the surrounding terrain. Flying low limits maneuverability since valleys are narrower at lower points. It's also necessary to control speed, keeping it close to the minimum maneuvering speed, which gives you better control of the plane. In many cases, pilots tend to pull the yoke back excessively, bringing the plane close to or into stall speed. At this point, it's also important to consider wind direction. For instance, a tailwind could reduce climb capability and increase ground speed.

Once the situation has been assessed, choose the point to begin the turn carefully, looking for the widest possible section or any opening in the slope that provides more room to maneuver.

There are several maneuvers that can be applied in mountain flying. Each of them is best practiced in a safe environment. During our time in Cholila, we received many pilots from various backgrounds and experience levels. But I was surprised to find that several of them didn't know their aircraft's turning radius. In the plains, they had never needed to know, and the lack of visual references contributed to this. Many of them entered the wide expanse of Lake Cholila, enclosed between two large mountains, yet hesitated, unsure if they could turn within it.

Successfully executing a 180-degree turn in a mountainous environment depends not only on technique but also on the ability to anticipate problems, knowing your plane well, and staying calm under pressure. Practicing this maneuver in a controlled environment is essential to building the confidence and skill necessary to perform it safely in a real situation.

Spiral Climb

The spiral climb is a maneuver that can be highly useful when it is necessary to gain altitude quickly and efficiently within a confined horizontal space. To begin, before performing the maneuver, it's essential to evaluate the surrounding terrain, ensuring there are no immediate obstacles that could interfere with the aircraft's path. Also, consider the topography to plan the best ascent route and avoid surprises during the maneuver.

During the climb, maintaining a clear visual reference is crucial for spatial orientation. In mountainous environments, it is easy to lose a sense of direction, especially in marginal visibility conditions. If visual references are insufficient, the plane's instruments become a primary guide—a GPS is particularly helpful in these situations. After completing the first full turn safely, it's possible to follow the marked track, ensuring the aircraft remains directly above the chosen point.

It's important to establish a climb speed that provides a good margin above stall speed to maintain precise control of the aircraft. Generally, you should select a speed slightly higher than the normal climb speed to ensure that additional safety margin.

With the aircraft correctly configured and the maneuver area established, increase power to maintain a stable climb rate and prevent altitude loss during the turn. In many cases, this will involve applying maximum power or close to it, providing the thrust needed to quickly gain altitude. The oil and cylinder head temperature may increase, but it's preferable to this than risking an error in maneuvering.

The turn should be made smoothly, banking the aircraft 20 to 30 degrees while keeping the nose slightly elevated—enough to balance between an efficient turn radius and the lift needed for the climb. Once the best climb rate is determined while maintaining the spiral, the turn should be uniform in terms of bank, power, direction, and speed. In some cases, if the valley widens with altitude, the turn radius can be gradually increased, with a shallower bank to maximize lift and climbing efficiency.

Throughout the maneuver, it's essential to monitor speed closely to avoid a stall, correcting with power or reducing the angle of attack to maintain safe speed and perform a coordinated turn. Proper use of rudder and ailerons avoids slips or skids that could complicate the maneuver and reduce the efficiency of the climb.

Finally, upon reaching the desired altitude, exit the spiral gradually, reducing bank, leveling off, and adjusting power to a cruise or level flight configuration. Also, readjust the flight direction to align with the planned route.

It's important to consider that as altitude increases, air density decreases, affecting both engine performance and aircraft lift. This means that at higher altitudes, the maneuver may require more space or a lower bank angle to avoid loss of lift. Additionally, make the appropriate mixture adjustments for altitude.

The maneuver requires a combination of precision, control, and a deep understanding of the environment in which it's performed. When executed correctly, it allows for safe navigation over complex terrain to reach secure altitudes, even within the tight limits imposed by the mountains.

Steep Turns

Steep turns are commonly used in mountain flying, especially in narrow valleys where it's necessary to reverse course. In these circumstances, options for changing direction or gaining altitude are quite limited, and any error could have serious consequences.

The goal of a steep turn is to allow the pilot to change direction quickly and accurately without covering a large horizontal distance. This maneuver is used to avoid an obstacle or to align the aircraft with a new route within a confined space. Unlike gentle turns performed in other types of flight, steep turns require greater bank and more precise control of the aircraft due to the restricted environment in which they are executed.

Before initiating a steep turn, ensure the aircraft is flying at an adequate speed. This speed must be sufficient to support the increased lift demand due to the bank and withstand a higher G-load. The risk of entering a stall increases, which is especially dangerous in an environment where there is limited room for recovery maneuvers.

With the aircraft stabilized, the pilot should position the plane as close to one edge of the canyon as safety allows and initiate the turn by decisively banking the wings to the opposite side. This bank angle, which can reach or exceed 45 degrees, characterizes a steep turn. The sharp angle allows the plane to turn quickly, minimizing horizontal travel in the limited space.

This increased bank angle also reduces lift, which can cause a nose-down motion and altitude loss if not properly compensated. To counteract this loss of lift, the pilot must increase engine thrust while beginning the turn. This additional power helps maintain level flight and prevents the aircraft from descending, especially in mountainous environments where terrain can rise quickly. If the terrain drops away behind, a nose-down motion is permissible to maintain speed.

This speed must be closely monitored to prevent a stall, which could lead to a hazardous situation, and to avoid side slips or skids that could destabilize the aircraft.

Once the turn reaches the desired angle and the new flight direction is established, the pilot should exit the turn with the same precision used to enter it. This involves gradually

- En los valles debemos volar a una velocidad y altitud seguras intentando volar pegado a una ladera, ascendente si la hubiera.
- → Asegurarse que el valle en el que se ingresa tiene salida y no acabe en un circo! ←
- Si el valle se va estrechando vigilar de tener suficiente amplitud para virar y poder salir.
- La pendiente no debe superar el régimen de ascenso, si la velocidad decae demasiado en el ascenso virar al valle.

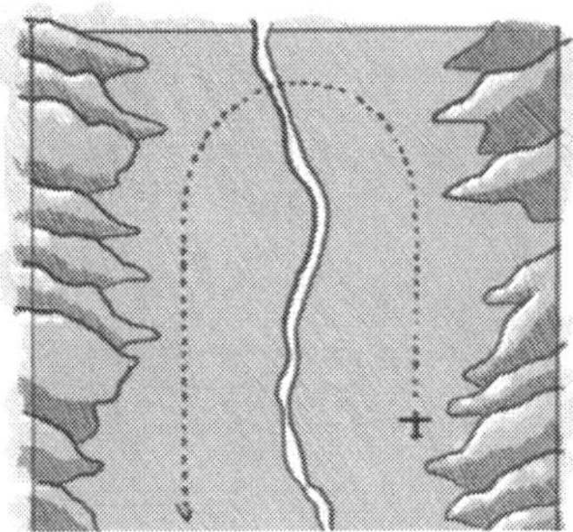

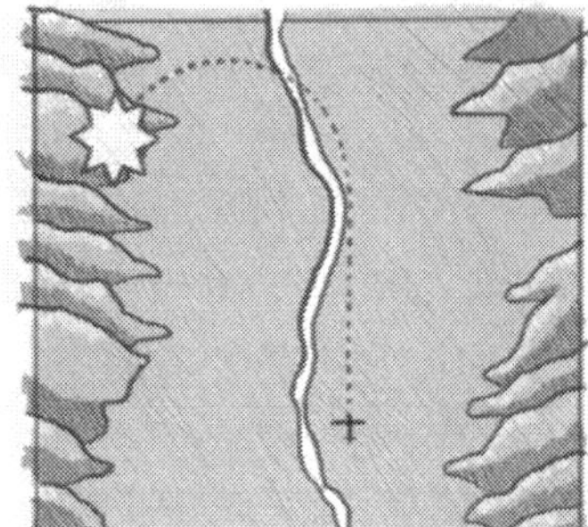

reducing the bank angle while adjusting engine power to return to a normal flight configuration. The turn's exit must be smooth and controlled, as any sudden movement could destabilize the plane, particularly in mountainous terrain with little room for corrective action.

Mountains create complex and changing air currents, with updrafts and downdrafts that can significantly impact the aircraft's performance during a turn. When flying close to a slope, downdrafts that reduce lift may be encountered at the critical moment of the turn. In such cases, the pilot must be able to adjust bank and power quickly to compensate for these variations.

Another important consideration is proximity to terrain. In mountains, it's easy to underestimate the closeness of a slope or the speed with which the terrain can change. The pilot must always be aware of their position relative to the terrain and anticipate how changes in topography could affect the maneuver.

Even a slight deviation in direction or altitude during a steep turn can lead to a dangerous situation if not corrected immediately.

The success of a steep turn in a mountainous environment largely depends on the pilot's ability to manage multiple variables simultaneously. This includes precise control of speed, bank, and power, as well as the ability to anticipate and react to air currents and terrain changes. Mastering steep turns requires dedicated training and consistent practice in various conditions. Pilots must become familiar with how their aircraft responds to different flight configurations and learn to make fine adjustments under pressure. Mastering this maneuver provides security and confidence to pilots navigating constrained spaces where they may face critical situations.

Chandelle

The chandelle is a maximum-performance climbing turn. It's a classic maneuver in aviation, combining a turn with a steep climb, allowing the pilot to change direction effectively while gaining altitude in a confined space.

In addition to mastering the technique under normal flight conditions, it's also important to practice it at higher altitudes, where engine performance and the aircraft's aerodynamics may differ. At high altitudes, where the air is less dense, the aircraft may respond differently, and engine power may be less effective, requiring fine adjustments by the pilot to execute the chandelle safely and effectively.

The maneuver begins from straight and level flight. The pilot starts banking the aircraft to one side (usually with a bank angle between 30 and 40 degrees) while simultaneously applying full power and beginning a climb. As the maneuver progresses, the pilot must maintain constant power, pushing the engine to maximum to provide the thrust needed to sustain the climb.

During the first half of the maneuver, the aircraft continues to climb while maintaining a steady rate of turn. As the maneuver progresses and the bank angle is maintained, the aircraft loses speed. The pilot must constantly adjust the ailerons, rudder, and elevator to control the bank angle and avoid a loss of lift.

At the halfway point of the turn, the bank angle is gradually reduced while keeping the nose of the aircraft pointed upward. The aircraft's speed begins to decrease naturally due to the increased angle of attack and aerodynamic drag associated with the climb. Here is where the chandelle differs from other climbing maneuvers, as it allows the speed to decrease gradually until it reaches a minimum safe flying speed.

This adjustment allows the aircraft to continue gaining altitude, albeit at a slower rate, while completing the turn. Finally, before the aircraft reaches stall speed, the pilot must level the wings and adjust the power, allowing the plane to return to straight and level flight in the new direction, having gained significant altitude during the maneuver. At the end of the chandelle, the aircraft will be on a new heading, having completed a roughly 180-degree turn with the nose level and reduced speed.

This combination of turning and climbing makes the chandelle an effective maneuver when altitude gain is needed without covering much horizontal distance.

Half-Turn Maneuver (Wingover)

The half-turn, known in aviation as a "wingover," is an advanced 180-degree heading change maneuver that enables the pilot to quickly modify the flight path at a steep angle. This technique borders on the acrobatic and requires precise control of the aircraft and effective coordination of the command systems.

The maneuver begins with a climbing turn, progressively increasing the bank angle while maintaining a speed higher than typical cruise speed. Whenever space and conditions allow, it's advisable to start with a descent to gain energy and ensure a sufficient speed reserve for the maneuver. As the aircraft ascends, the angle increases until, at the maneuver's apex, it nears the stall point. The aircraft's nose begins to drop naturally, changing heading with the support of the inside rudder, while the ailerons and elevator remain neutral. During the descent, the pilot carefully adjusts power and bank angle, avoiding excessive altitude loss or unwanted acceleration, ensuring a smooth, controlled descent towards the opposite heading.

As the aircraft regains altitude, it levels off into straight and stable flight, now in the opposite direction from the original course. In certain cases, it may be necessary to apply slight opposite rudder to stabilize the flight path. Although it appears simple, this maneuver requires precision and coordination, as each phase depends on the proper synchronization of controls and constant attention to both the surroundings and flight indicators.

Upon completing the turn, the pilot should reassess whether the new heading offers a safe escape route or if it is necessary to continue climbing or plan an emergency landing in an appropriate area.

Ridge Crossing

The Andes Mountain Range is one of the longest mountain formations on the planet, extending along the western coast of South America from the Llanos region in Venezuela in the north to southern Chile and Argentina, spanning Colombia, Ecuador, Peru, Bolivia, Chile, and Argentina, down to Tierra del Fuego in the south. The entire range covers approximately 8,000 kilometers, of which just over 5,000 km are shared by Argentina and Chile, forming a natural border between the two countries.

The width of the range varies along its length, from around 200 kilometers in some sections to over 700 kilometers in others. The average altitude of the Andes ranges between 3,000 and 4,000 meters (9,800 and 13,100 feet) above sea level, though some peaks reach much greater heights.

The Andes is geologically young, with its formation beginning approximately 65 million years ago, toward the end of the late Cretaceous period, coinciding with the final phase of the Mesozoic era. Its morphology is diverse, presenting a mix of high peaks, such as Mount Aconcagua, the tallest peak in the Americas, vast plateaus like the Andean Altiplano, and deep valleys that run between the major mountain chains.

Flying along the Andes from north to south, pilots encounter continuous mountain ridges branching from the main range, with transverse valleys that lead to the Atlantic slopes (mainly in Argentina) to the east and the Pacific slopes (mainly in Chile) to the west.

If the flight plan doesn't follow valleys beneath high peaks, it often requires crossing these transverse ridges with sharply defined, jagged crests featuring steep profiles—a characteristic attributed to the Andes' geological youth, in contrast to older ranges that have been smoothed and rounded by millions of years of erosion.

This terrain can be intimidating, as if the flight level isn't high enough, the mountains may appear to rise suddenly, casting doubt on whether they can be crossed. Therefore, it's essential to study the intended route and the height of these mountain obstacles beforehand.

When flying from La Esperanza to Cholila, there are three

possible routes depending on the weather, especially wind and cloud cover. The longest route goes via Lake Puelo and around Cerro Epuyén, over Lake Epuyén, and then emerging at Lake Lezana. This route is used when the cloud ceiling is low, as the aircraft won't need to cross any mountain ridges except for the elevation separating Lakes Epuyén and Puelo. If clouds prevent this crossing, it's still possible, albeit on a longer route, to fly north around Cerro Pirke over the town of El Hoyo and then south through a narrow valley over a road, passing Laguna Las Mercedes on the left on a southerly course.

A second and more commonly used route crosses above Cerro Plataforma, which separates the valleys of the Puelo and Tigre Rivers, the latter being the main tributary of Lake Cholila. On the Puelo side, the winds are favorable for climbing. From the base of the broad valley where the Turbio River flows west to east, the wind flows practically unobstructed until it encounters Cerro Plataforma, El Derrumbe, and, finally, Tres Picos. This configuration facilitates a relatively smooth climb. Cerro Plataforma has a flat surface where the wind tends to behave in a laminar manner; however, it ends in an abrupt cliff, and the air follows the terrain, creating a significant, turbulent downdraft on the leeward side due to the convergence of winds from various directions. Despite this, the descent can be calculated since the terrain is relatively low and provides enough space for this transition. After a brief stretch, you reach Lake Cholila, where the airflow is unidirectional and steady.

This route is challenging in the opposite direction, and it's essential to gain enough altitude to counteract the downdrafts until reaching the peak of the mountain.

A third route is only used on very calm, clear days. It's the most direct but also riskier, as it requires flying very close to the mountains and descending through a narrow valley along the Arroyo del Turco on the northern face of Cerro Tres Picos.

This crossing demands precise flying technique, as the first obstacle to overcome is Cerro El Derrumbe, which presents a well-defined ridge perpendicular to the flight path. Depending on the day's weather conditions or the aircraft's weight and balance, it may not be possible to reach the altitude necessary to clear it. For this reason, a recommended technique—applicable in similar situations—is to approach the mountain flying parallel and as close as safely possible, while maintaining a steady climb rate. This allows the pilot to assess the relative height of the mountain and determine if it's safe to cross without risk. Once the ridge line is clearly below the flight horizon, level the plane, increase speed, and proceed with a controlled crossing.

To avoid misleading distortions, it's crucial to level the aircraft before deciding to cross. In a climbing attitude, the pitch angle can distort the pilot's perception, especially at high altitudes or with limited visual references. This could lead to a dangerous misjudgment. The pilot should rely on flight instruments, properly adjust power, reduce the angle of attack to avoid an excessive pitch attitude, and interpret the terrain references objectively, avoiding reliance solely on physical sensations.

Some indicators can help assess whether the aircraft has reached a safe altitude to cross. One is to observe mountain lakes, which act as natural level references. From a higher position, these bodies of water should be fully visible, showing a clear difference between the near and far shorelines. This suggests that the aircraft is above the lake level, and projecting this reference laterally toward the mountain pass can determine with high certainty if the altitude is sufficient.

Another useful technique is to analyze the landscape

beyond the mountain barrier. If the terrain on the opposite side gradually disappears as you approach the ridge, it indicates insufficient altitude. Conversely, if the terrain on the other side becomes more visible, it signals that the aircraft is flying above the crest and the crossing can be performed safely.

Once level, increase speed, preferably above cruise speed, to provide a greater safety margin against a potential loss of lift, typically caused by unpredictable and difficult-to-read winds at this position. If the aircraft flies too slowly, any sudden change in wind direction or strength could drastically reduce lift and create a dangerous condition. Increased speed offers an additional safety margin, keeping the aircraft above its stall speed even in unstable conditions.

Approaching the crossing at a 45° angle provides a better escape option if the maneuver needs to be reversed. If issues arise on the other side—such as a sharp downdraft, lack of visibility, or an unknown obstacle that cannot be cleared, or even a potential engine failure at such a critical point at the mountain's highest point—attempting the crossing this way means that a quick, short turn can return the plane to the valley. Approaching straight on and aborting the crossing would require a full heading reversal, taking more time, space, and providing less safety.

Once over the crest and with a complete view of the other side, it's advisable to realign the aircraft perpendicular to the mountain, not only for a faster exit but also to situate it over the valley in a comfortable attitude to manage any potential emergency, but now on the opposite side. It's best to choose a section of the ridge with a knife-edge shape instead of a flat or rounded crest, which requires more time to cross.

If there is some wind and dynamic lift, flying at a 45° angle keeps the aircraft climbing longer relative to the airflow, which helps maintain kinetic energy and control. Once sufficient altitude is ensured, turning 90° can take advantage of the updrafts often found just above the ridge, helping to maintain altitude without needing a steep climb. However, be mindful of the leeward side's downdrafts.

In this phase, it's important to be prepared to counter any altitude loss by increasing engine power as necessary. Finally, after completing the crossing, it's essential to stay vigilant and be ready for any sudden changes in flight conditions, prepared to make quick decisions to ensure flight safety.

Therefore, it's essential to seriously consider the wind factor, which plays a significant role in ridge crossings. Ideally, the pilot should approach from the windward side, where the wind meets the mountain and is forced upward as it hits the slope, creating updrafts that can be used to gain altitude. This can help sustain the aircraft and provide the additional lift needed to clear the ridge more safely. However, if the wind is too strong, it may generate severe turbulence and rotors at the ridge and on the leeward side.

Although it may extend the flight, prudence suggests flying parallel to the ridge on the windward side until reaching a sufficient altitude or a safer point to attempt the crossing. Adequate altitude provides increased safety and offers a better perspective of the surrounding terrain, allowing a more accurate assessment of wind conditions. The pilot should observe indicators such as trees, smoke, or lake surfaces to gauge real speed, direction, intensity, and wind behavior, to develop a crossing strategy.

Once the crossing is decided, be prepared to encounter downdrafts on the other side, so ensure you have an energy reserve in speed to counteract this. This means flying at a speed sufficient to allow some maneuvering margin if the aircraft encounters a sudden drop.

Air Mass Movement

In all cases, gaining altitude provides greater distance from the mountain and its influence on air movement, considering that wind speed can increase significantly as one ascends. These changes are strongly influenced by the interaction between the wind and the topography and specific terrain characteristics.

At ground level, especially in valleys and on the lower slopes of mountains, wind is typically slower. This is largely due to friction from the terrain, which includes not only the surface itself but also natural obstacles such as trees, rocks, and buildings. These features act as brakes, reducing wind speed in lower areas. However, as one rises above these obstacles, the friction influence decreases, allowing the wind to accelerate. Further from the irregularities of the terrain, the wind becomes more laminar and less turbulent. If this wind has a favorable component, it can provide a smoother, faster flying experience.

In these lower levels, a phenomenon known as wind channeling often occurs through narrow valleys or gorges. As it flows through these confined spaces, the wind is forced to accelerate, creating an effect similar to the Venturi principle, where the flow of a fluid speeds up when passing through a narrower section.

In addition to this channeling effect, mountains are prone to generating meteorological phenomena known as mountain waves. These waves form when strong wind hits a mountain range perpendicularly and is forced to rise, creating a series of standing waves in the atmosphere. These waves can extend vertically to great heights and can cause significant variations in wind speed at different altitudes. At the crests of these waves, the wind may accelerate drastically, while at the troughs, it may decrease. For pilots, these waves can be both a challenge and an opportunity: they can take advantage of the updrafts to gain altitude but must also be prepared for severe turbulence and abrupt changes in wind speed that can accompany this movement.

It's always prudent to have an alternate route in mind in case conditions make crossing a crest safely impossible. These alternate routes may include adjacent valleys or lower paths that offer a less risky crossing.

A less common, but occasionally present phenomenon in mountainous areas is thermal inversion, where a layer of warmer air is situated above a layer of cooler air. Unlike normal atmospheric conditions, where temperature decreases as altitude increases, a thermal inversion creates an unusual, stable atmospheric structure that inhibits vertical air movement and prevents mixing between the air layers.

As a result, winds in this lower layer tend to be light or even absent, and the air feels calm and stable. This can change wind dynamics, with lower wind speeds within the inversion layer, but a sharp increase in speed above it, where the warmer, less dense air interacts with faster, more turbulent winds. A pilot ascending from a calm wind environment can suddenly encounter very strong and turbulent winds above this layer.

Thermal inversion also has other important implications. By creating a stable layer of cold air trapped in valleys, it can trap clouds and smoke at lower levels, which can significantly reduce visibility. During the day, especially on cold mornings, it is common to see a layer of fog or smog near the ground, while the air at higher altitudes is clear and bright.

Therefore, this phenomenon not only influences wind speed but can also affect air stability, visibility, and overall flight safety. Recognizing and managing it is essential for safe navigation in mountainous areas.

CHAPTER 2
SURVIVAL IN THE MOUNTAINS

"Patagonia is the land where stones fly." This is how Antoine de Saint-Exupéry referred to this region while boarding his Laté 25 airplane. He had flown over the sea, the Sahara Desert, and other dangerous routes, but he considered flights to Patagonia as those presenting the greatest challenge. His airplane was a robust aircraft, capable of operating under difficult conditions, especially important for air routes over rugged terrain and severe weather. It was designed as a mail and light transport plane and was built by the French company Latécoère in the 1920s. His experience with this airplane and these missions deeply influenced his literary work and his romantic and philosophical view of flight and the solitude of the pilot facing the challenges of the air and nature.

Aeroposta had a route to Santiago de Chile, crossing the Andes. On March 2, 1929, his colleague Jean Mermoz, with a twin aircraft, was caught by a downdraft and forced to land on a mountain plateau 300 meters wide at an altitude of 4,000 meters. With his mechanic, Alexandre Collenot, and the passenger, Count Henry de La Vaulx, Mermoz spent the next four days repairing and lightening the plane, while also clearing a path to the edge of the precipice. Then, he taxied to the edge, diving the plane to gain speed and successfully reached Santiago.

Saint-Exupéry was not daunted by flying in these conditions. He was a great pilot, but above all, he was a poet of the air, and he found in the skies of Patagonia an ideal stage for his adventurous soul. Each takeoff filled him with a mixture of anticipation and reverence. He felt that every flight was a delicate dance between man and the elements, which deepened his respect for nature. And although it made him feel small, at the same time, it gave him a sense of belonging to something much greater than himself. Patagonia, with its raw beauty and harshness, became the mirror of his own soul, a reflection of his search for meaning and his longing to understand his place in the universe. The mountains, with their deep shadows and sunlit peaks, stood as silent witnesses to his meditations and dreams, which we later enjoy in his literary works.

It was in this solitude of flight where his deep reflections arose, finding clarity of thought and a serenity that only the vastness of the sky could offer. But, while on one hand it provided him a space for introspection and contemplation, on the other, it reminded him of the fragility of his existence and the constant threat of a fatal accident. Saint-Exupéry was fully aware that, in those moments of isolation, he depended entirely on his skill and the reliability of his aircraft.

Many pilots, even today, with more modern aircraft, advanced technology, and a better understanding of geography and its climatic variables, when flying in the Patagonian mountains, if they allow these transformative forces to permeate their spirit, will inevitably feel a mixture of awe, apprehension, and also fear.

The mountains, with their snow-capped peaks and deep valleys, not only offer a captivating landscape, but also present technical, skill, and emotional challenges, requiring a deep understanding of what it means to fly in such places. For these pilots, who often fly on isolated and less-traveled routes, the possibility of an emergency landing is an alternative that must be considered. And to recognize this means acknowledging that, in the event of a fortunate landing, there will be a time when survival techniques will need to be applied until rescue, which will hardly happen immediately.

If this were to happen, it is important to leave a record. When a pilot recounts their experiences from critical moments, it opens up a space for reflection on mistakes made, decisions taken, and strategies that worked or didn't work. This act of sharing is beneficial in strengthening a safety culture in aviation, where the priority is to prevent accidents and constantly improve flying practices.

Through these stories, a type of knowledge is shared that is rarely found in manuals, knowledge that comes from lived experience and offers lessons that might otherwise go unnoticed. The aim is for other pilots to learn from the experiences of others without having to face them directly, or, if they do, to develop their own criteria and strategies for dealing with the unexpected by listening to or reading about how their colleagues have managed moments of crisis. This not only enriches their training but also better prepares them to react calmly and effectively when fate presents a similar challenge.

The following account is part of this context.

Ezequiel "Queque" Parodi was very satisfied. Despite the little time we had, he had completed the flight objectives. A polar front was expected in the coming days, with heavy snowstorms forecasted by even the least credible forecasters, which would prevent him from returning to Esperanza. We were ready for the return. But fate had something else in store for us.

Queque tells it this way:

The work we had gone to do had turned out more than well. I had connected the two satellite internet antennas in both outposts at each end of the lake. Now they could communicate with each other and also with the world. There was little daylight left, and we still had to return to Trevelin, but I managed to test the camera placed at the end of the runway, which would allow me to check the weather conditions via the internet and even see if any animals were present. I couldn't configure it exactly as I'd have liked, but the day was short, and we couldn't afford to lose any more time if we wanted to reach our hangar before sunset. I'd finish it on another occasion later on.

Dany and Pablo were with me in their Cessna 180. They had helped transport part of the load. We taxied together to the opposite end of the runway. Dany went ahead to position himself behind me when we reversed direction to take off. To save time, and since my plane was slower and could take off in a very short distance, I decided to use only half of the runway and clear it quickly so the Cessna could take off comfortably.

"LV GBY is doing a 180 and taking off," I informed my flight companions. I turned toward the lake and applied power. What joy! As light as it was, as soon as I started rolling, the PA18 wanted to lift off, and I guided it upward with a vertical speed that few planes in this category can achieve—twelve hundred feet per minute! I savored the moment as I climbed, turning to reach the altitude that would allow me to pass over the mountain closing in on the Esperanza Lake valley. Beneath my wing, I could see that after a short takeoff run, the Cessna was also airborne.

Danny and Pablo quickly caught up to me and positioned themselves to my left. What a beautiful plane! I'd had it in my hangar for the past six months, and if it looked stunning on the ground, it looked even more impressive in the air, standing out against the green of the forest. I'd always admired its lines and its robustness, and Pablo's paint scheme design, inspired by "The Spirit of Columbus," the Cessna 180 with which Geraldine Mock circumnavigated the world solo, covering over 35,000 kilometers with 21 stops in 29 days, seemed incredibly fitting.

I also enjoyed flying it—powerful as all Cessna 180s are. I've tested several with the intent to purchase, but for some reason, I feel that this one flies the best.

I leveled off at 5,500 feet and noticed that my companions continued to 6,000 feet, where they encountered significant turbulence. They informed me over the radio, and knowing that their plane was heavier, I realized my Piper PA18 would be much more affected. Communication was good, so I let them know I'd descend a bit and cross through the middle of the mountain, over the lake, which was frozen and covered in snow, though the irregular edges of the shoreline stood out clearly.

Familiar with the area and having crossed that mountain under various weather conditions, I knew the air would be smoother at that trajectory and altitude. I checked my altimeter, which read 5,450 feet as I approached the northern cliff of Cerro Plataforma, a unique geological formation created by an uplifted seabed. Once over the lake, I initiated a gentle left turn to exit the mountain over the waterfalls of the stream draining this body of water to the south.

A depression formed there that made crossing easier when done at a lower altitude. Meanwhile, I looked up through the roof window for Pablo and Danny but didn't spot them on my first glance, which extended my search time.

The moment I directed my gaze forward, I found myself practically on top of the snow. When I realized this, I tried to climb, but my left wheel was already sinking into the deep layer of soft snow, and I felt the plane come to an abrupt stop. Everything happened so quickly—if I were to describe it in a comic strip, the next frame would have me upside down inside the plane.

Snow can be very treacherous. Expert skiers, unable to perceive shapes, are often surprised by small bumps or dips during a descent, forcing them to adjust. Without visual references, shapes and distances are hard to gauge. This also happens when flying over a mirrored lake; the sense of vertical distance disappears.

Pilots who fly with skis are well aware of this and keep it in mind. Don Sheldon, one of the pioneers in mountain flights and glacier landings, used to cut small spruce branches and throw them onto his improvised runways before landing, using them as reference points. When the sun is favorable, many also use the plane's shadow to determine their distance from the ground.

In snow, especially on sunless days, the light diffuses evenly in all directions, creating a monotonous landscape, eliminating shadows and the visible horizon, and generating a confusion known as "spatial disorientation."

Despite the shock of the moment, I didn't lose my sense of reality, time, or space. I was fully aware that I was overturned on the frozen lake, and my first thought was that the ice's thickness wouldn't withstand the impact or the weight of my plane, and that both of us would sink.

Immediately, I unfastened my seatbelt, opened the door, and quickly exited the cockpit. At the same time, I felt the wind hitting me, and an intense cold invaded my entire body. The door was open, and against my desire to escape, I grabbed my jacket and put it on right away. Meanwhile, I heard Dany's voice over the radio asking if I was okay. I took the helmet I had removed just moments before, equipped with a headset, and knowing how important it was to communicate my condition, I brought the microphone close to my mouth, searched for the PTT, making an effort to orient myself since the plane was upside down, and replied, "Dany, I'm okay, but I need to get out of here urgently." I let go of the helmet and grabbed the bag I had inside; meanwhile, I realized I had almost nothing that could help me. I had my computer, which I had used to install and configure the antennas, but my survival kit, which I always carry in the rear compartment, wasn't there—I remembered I'd removed it that morning to make room for cargo.

I had to overcome that feeling of discouragement. The priority now was to reach the shore in case the ice fractured. As I was pulling out the few things I had in the plane, I heard Dany on the radio again: "Queque, are you okay?" and I realized he hadn't heard me. I quickly looked for the cause of the communication issue. The radio master switch was on, but as I traced the path from the microphone capsule of my helmet to the radio, I saw that the microphone cable was unplugged. I swiftly reconnected the microphone and repeated my message: "I'm okay, but I need to get out of here urgently." At that moment, I realized I was standing on the underside of my wing, and it pained me to think that I was damaging the fabric of the plane I loved most—the plane that had always inspired me to become a pilot.

The Piper Super Cub had always been my inspiration. I used to watch videos of Alaskan Bush pilots on my computer and dreamed of becoming a pilot, flying a Super Cub in the mountains, doing the same work they did—helping and rescuing in remote areas, transporting supplies, medicines, and conducting rescues. There was no information that this type of flying existed in the country, and I saw no reason why it couldn't be developed. I wanted people to know about it, to see it; I wanted to bring this kind of aviation to life in Argentina. I saw similarities between that inhospitable northern region and Patagonia, where I lived.

With great effort, I managed to complete the private pilot course, traveling more than 600 km every time I wanted to fly since I had to go to Trelew, the nearest place where I could receive training.

I grabbed my helmet and put it on; I knew I needed to protect myself from any potential head injury. I was on a mountain with a fairly flat configuration in the area where I was, but it was surrounded by cliffs, very hard to descend, and I had very little time left. I climbed off the wing, always fearing I would hear the cracking of ice breaking beneath my feet. I thought that perhaps, with more surface area supporting it, the plane could stay on top of the snow-covered lake, but my foot would sink deeper into the ice, increasing the risk and the likelihood of breaking it, and I had no idea how thick it might be.

I began to walk laboriously toward the shore; I was already soaked up to my waist and couldn't stop thinking about the possibility of the ice breaking. I fixed my gaze on a point on the shore and didn't even look back to see the plane.

Meanwhile, I could hear the sound of the Cessna's engine circling above me, and I felt it might mask the noise of the ice breaking. At the same time, I knew that hearing it in advance wouldn't help; inevitably, I would sink into the depths. There would be no way out. Nonetheless, I focused on a point on the shore and headed towards it as quickly as the depth of the snow allowed, as I was sinking well above my knees. At the same time, I tried not to impact the ground forcefully, as if that could somehow help keep the surface of the ice intact.

Time seemed to slow down. Every step was drenched in slowness. I kept my eyes on the shore, and it felt like I would never get there. I don't know how long it took me to get out. But as I took the last step off the snow-covered ice, fully aware that I was finally out, I turned around and saw my PA18 overturned, wheels pointing to the sky, and my trail in the snow leading in a straight line to where I stood. It felt like a dream I wanted to wake up from. I couldn't believe I was living through this situation—my beloved plane was upside down, almost in the center of the lake, with the ice possibly breaking, sinking, and maybe never being recoverable. My mind shot to one thought: I had to get it out of there quickly. But as if reality slapped me, I looked around. The perfectly flat surface with the plane like an ornament stood out starkly. The concavity of the surroundings was also very clear.

Surviving in the mountains under conditions of snow, ice, and wind is a complex discipline that combines technical knowledge, practical skills, and a resilient mindset. Snow can be both an ally and an adversary. In this case, it trapped him and caused the plane to overturn, but the quantity and texture cushioned the impact, reducing the damage to the plane and, on the other hand, preventing Queque from getting hurt.

However, it's worth noting that he was wearing a harness, which kept him from slamming into the dashboard and control stick during the abrupt stop. Moreover, whenever he flies the PA18, he always wears a helmet, which dampens external noise, holds his headset, and protects his head, as in this case. Upon examination, the helmet showed a scuffed area where it had clearly struck something.

The Cessna flew by much lower, helping me reorient myself in time and space. My mind was working, assessing the situation. I saw Dany approaching in a slow flight, with a notch of flaps, and Pablo half out of the plane, holding something to throw down to me. They passed over me, and I saw a backpack fall. I immediately knew what it was; I was familiar with Dany's survival kit, as we had given talks and made videos showcasing his gear, and as I watched it fall, I expressed my gratitude to them. What was in that backpack greatly changed my outlook on enduring what lay ahead.

I immediately recalled the flour bomb competitions we did in Trevelin and felt a sense of pride that we practiced this kind of skill. Dany and I had also dropped supplies to isolated residents during heavy snowfalls.

I understood that they had waited for me to reach the shore so they wouldn't drop it on the ice, and I could see and retrieve it safely. I took the backpack, lifted it, signaling that I had it, and watched as they turned and headed toward El Bolsón. I knew and trusted that they would initiate a rescue operation. I transferred the contents of my bag into the backpack to continue with only one load.

Once the backpack was dropped and Queque confirmed he had it, we set off at full power toward El Bolsón. We had confidence in Queque because he knew the mountains. Simply carrying a survival kit is not enough; the key is knowing how to use each item effectively under pressure. The same equipment in another person's hands wouldn't guarantee proper use. This account aims to combine technical knowledge with instructive experiences and examples from real-life situations, so it may be useful to others who might face a similar situation.

An interesting precedent of a nearly analogous situation, albeit on a different scale, involved a plane from Aeroposta Argentina S.A. On July 8, 1946, in the dead of winter, the Aeroposta Argentina S.A. Junkers JU-52 Ibaté crashed on the plateau of Lake Buenos Aires (in the northwest of what is now the Province of Santa Cruz). The snow cushioned the impact and prevented a tragedy; the plane was damaged, but the cabin remained intact, serving as a shelter for the survivors. Despite communication challenges, the radio telegrapher was able to provide their position. The next day, they were found in the middle of the inhospitable plateau of Lake Buenos Aires by the crew of the plane Quichua, another Junkers Ju 52 from the same company. Facing adverse weather conditions, the Quichua flew over the crash site to drop food and warm clothing to the people trapped below.

To ensure the survivors' survival, carefully prepared packages with a variety of supplies were dropped from the air. Among the food items were canned goods, bread, crackers, dried fruits, nuts, sugar, and powdered milk. These non-perishable, energy-dense items were essential for keeping the survivors nourished in the harsh conditions of the terrain.

In addition to food, items were also dropped to protect the people from the intense cold characteristic of the region. Blankets, warm clothing, sleeping bags, boots, and gloves were provided. These items aimed to keep the survivors warm and protect them from the low temperatures during their time exposed to the elements.

After four days, a ground patrol arrived and guided them to the edge of the plateau. Meanwhile, the other plane continued accompanying them and dropping supplies.

Later, the survivors' testimonies revealed that this effort was not only vital for their survival—providing food and shelter—but also offered hope and support in a moment of great need.

As I listened to the roar of the Cessna fading away, a feeling of loneliness and abandonment began to creep in. Now, it was up to me alone to survive until I was rescued. I wished the Cessna had had skis, like the ones I'd seen in Alaska less than a month ago. It would have been so easy. They'd land on the shore, I'd climb into the plane, and soon we'd be enjoying a hot coffee in a cabin, sitting by a lit fireplace.

But I had to stay focused. I mentally assessed the situation. This mountain is completely surrounded by cliffs; I'd flown over it hundreds of times, and I had to find a way down. The wind was picking up, there was very little daylight left, and I was at 5,000 feet on a snow-covered plateau I had never walked across and whose terrain I didn't know. What I did know was that there was no visible connection to the surrounding mountains. It's like an island in the sky.

I remembered that my friends Pablo, Tinti, and Guille had reached this place on foot. I had to find that access route and make my way down to the forest, a place where I could build a shelter and start a fire. Meanwhile, I thought about possible ways I could be rescued. My thoughts turned to my colleagues in the National Gendarmerie, Aviation Section of Trevelin. They had been without their B3 helicopter for a long time now—a helicopter I used to admire next to my first plane, the Cessna 152, when I started flying. This group of people and their hangar had been the first home for my planes and had supported my early steps in aviation. I had 12 gendarme friends whom I knew would immediately come to rescue me without hesitation if they had a helicopter. But that wasn't going to happen; it had been a long time since they'd had any flying machine in their beautiful hangar.

On the other hand, I was acutely aware that I didn't have the right equipment for where I was, and my worst enemy would be the hypothermic "monster," for which I had a healthy respect from years of winter activities in Patagonia. I had spent many days in the mountains, in the snow, mainly snowboarding, filming documentaries, building ramps, camping, and exploring places that taught me a lot about snow and survival.

That knowledge drove me to act, to make decisions, realizing that my wet feet in such low temperatures needed to keep moving. It was essential to find shelter from that harsh, icy wind that was freezing my pants, making them stiff and uncomfortable for walking, and even causing abrasions on my legs from the friction.

I knew I had to keep moving and not stop. While the body is engaged in physical activity, it generates heat, which melts the snow and ice sticking to the fabric, turning everything damp. But this moisture gravitates downward, soaking socks first, filling the shoes with cold water. As I walked, I looked around for a sheltered spot out of the wind, but Cerro Plataforma offers little shelter around the lake.

Queque was right; his battle now was against the cold. He had to find a shelter, but this was a flat, exposed plateau. He had to get out of there before the light faded and build a shelter.

Hypothermia is a medical condition that occurs when the body's temperature drops below normal levels, impairing the function of vital organs and bodily systems. This drop in temperature results from heat loss faster than the body can produce it, often due to prolonged exposure to cold environments.

When a person is exposed to low temperatures, the body initially responds with mechanisms to conserve heat. One of the first is peripheral vasoconstriction, which reduces blood flow to the skin and extremities to limit heat loss, helping to retain warmth in the core organs. Additionally, the body increases its metabolic rate and produces shivering, which are rapid muscle contractions designed to generate heat.

As body temperature continues to drop, these mechanisms become less effective. Brain function begins to deteriorate, manifesting as confusion, disorientation, and difficulty coordinating movements. The body's ability to maintain vasoconstriction is also compromised, and in some cases, people experience a "paradoxical undressing," where they feel a false warmth and remove their clothes, exacerbating heat loss. Queque, being a man of the snow, knew this condition; it was a moment of comfort that many would surrender to and fall asleep. It took a great effort of control to resist it. But giving in meant death.

In moderate to severe hypothermia, cardiovascular function is severely affected. Heart rate and blood pressure decrease, and bradycardia can occur, meaning the heart beats more slowly. At this stage, cardiac arrhythmias can also develop, which can be potentially life-threatening. Breathing becomes shallow and slow, reducing tissue oxygenation and potentially leading to dangerously low levels of oxygen in the blood (hypoxemia).

As the temperature continues to fall, kidney function deteriorates, which can lead to a decrease in urine production and the accumulation of toxins in the body. Blood clotting is also affected, increasing the risk of bleeding. If no action is taken to counteract the cooling of the body, the person may lose consciousness and eventually experience respiratory and cardiac arrest.

The treatment of hypothermia involves the gradual rewarming of the body. This is crucial to avoid complications like "rewarming shock," where a rapid increase in core temperature can trigger cardiovascular issues. The rewarming must be careful and controlled, possibly including the use of warm blankets, warmed intravenous fluids, and in severe cases, advanced methods like extracorporeal circulation. Additionally, it is essential to provide appropriate life support, such as oxygen therapy and cardiopulmonary resuscitation if necessary.

My primary decision was to head toward Cholila, and I began to circle the lake to try to descend on the southern side. However, when I reached the edge, I realized that descending there was impossible. I tried to find the most obvious path to start descending from that place and noticed that the terrain configuration was very different from what I'd encountered on

Cerro La Torta, Cerro Cónico, and Paso de Las Nubes.

As I was thinking this, I once again heard the unmistakable and familiar sound of the Cessna 180's Continental engine. I saw it making a turn over the mountain, and immediately, they spotted me. My tracks were very clear in the snow. Once again, they prepared for a low pass. I saw them slow down, and I saw Pablo leaning out of the window with a package. They dropped it, landing very close to me. Clearly, the practice we'd had in the flour bomb competitions was useful in cases like this.

They made a 360-degree turn to make sure I picked up the box. I hadn't expected them to return; there was very little daylight left. I signaled with my arms that I was heading toward Cholila, and I felt they understood me.

I felt a bit more at ease. They had seen me, they knew I was okay, and with some luck, they had understood where I was heading. I walked to a sheltered spot behind a snow-covered rock and opened both the backpack and the second package. This was a cardboard box containing chocolates, cereal bars, sugar candies, energy drinks, electrolyte drinks, lighters, and three jackets wrapped with a long rope. It was moving to see its contents. The jackets would help me fight the cold, and I immediately recognized one of them. Pablo and I had bought it not long ago at a shop in Alaska. I'd use the rope to hang clothes by the fire. But I didn't have much time to inspect it all. My body now had fuel, and I needed to act. I took one of the bottles of liquid, a cereal bar, and set out to find shelter.

But I was increasingly aware of how challenging my situation was. Dany and Pablo had watched me walk a fair distance before they left, so they would know I was okay, or at least understand that I was physically intact. But what I needed was a rescue, and with nightfall approaching and no helicopter involved, getting out of this place was going to be very difficult.

Even though twilight in the mountains lasts longer than on the plains once the sun sets, I had to act quickly. I was tired, my steps were much slower, and I began to feel that if I didn't descend from that mountain quickly, I would have to spend the night on the plateau, completely exposed and with that relentless wind beating against me. But if it came to that, I would have to make myself as comfortable as possible.

Finally, I found a place where the descent was relatively safe, though I was very wary of avalanches. I had taken courses on the subject, and I could tell that the snow on the slope was unstable; in fact, my descent caused small snow slides under my feet.

The cold wind was annoying, discouraging; I almost gave it a personality, as if it were a malevolent being, constantly reminding me of the vulnerable situation I was in. Every time it stopped blowing, even if only for a moment, it was like a weight lifted off me.

With the last rays of light, I spotted a large rock that wasn't completely exposed to the wind but provided more shelter than the area I was in. Although the wind varied in intensity there, there were moments when it stopped entirely. Additionally, there was a dry tree, so I immediately decided that this would be the place to spend the night. I couldn't risk sliding down a slope or triggering an avalanche. I would set up a bivouac with the orange plastic sheet I found in Dany's survival kit and try to make a fire to dry my clothes and keep warm. I knew that, with the little remaining daylight, I couldn't expect any help until the next day.

I tried to tie the rope at the top of the tree to break off

Laguna del plataforma
- Accidente -
Lugar del rescate

a relatively thin branch, but when I approached, I sank almost up to my neck, as blown snow had accumulated heavily on the side of the tree. I decided not to insist and looked for another thinner tree. I gathered some branches for firewood. I took off my helmet and began digging a snow cave and clearing an area for the fire.

Building a snow shelter is a technique taught in all mountain survival courses. The key is to choose a suitable location, preferably a gentle slope with enough snow, far from potential dangers like avalanches or fallen branches.

Inside the shelter, it's essential to insulate the ground to prevent heat loss. This can be done by placing a layer of branches, clothing, or any available insulating material. The entrance should be partially sealed with snow or equipment to retain heat, without completely blocking access to maintain ventilation.

Staying warm is paramount. It's important to avoid sweating and stay dry; if possible, change wet clothes for dry garments. In some cases, a small heat source, such as a camping heater, can help, as long as there's adequate ventilation to avoid hazards.

When I wasn't moving, I felt myself getting colder, so I opened my backpack to look for the sleeping bag and thermal bag. I had the same items in my own gear, which was now resting in my office in Trevelin. But I was grateful that Dany was also experienced in the mountains, being the son of a great explorer like Don Roy Wegrzyn, and understood which items were essential for a survival kit.

The thermal bag helps to retain the heat generated by one's own body. It's silver on the inside and orange on the outside. I decided to remove my wet pants and socks and get inside this bag as the first layer to conserve heat, then wrap my legs with the thickest jacket I had, which was the one Dany had been wearing and had thrown to me on the second drop. I wrapped my waist with another jacket, and finally, I took off my wet pants and socks and got into the thermal bag, then into the sleeping bag. As a final layer, I used the nylon bag to prevent the outside snow from soaking me.

Once inside the bag, I tried to make a fire. I took the fire starter from Dany's backpack, which seemed to be a yellow gel alcohol, along with a lighter, and set out to light a fire. I tried for two hours before giving up. The fire starter couldn't overcome the moisture in the wood; I used the cardboard from the box they had thrown to me and a few pages from the flight manual. I cut small pieces of nylon rope. The only flame I managed to get lasted a few minutes, and it was absolutely insufficient to dry my clothes. Once the cardboard box and the flammable liquid were used up, I was left without a heat source and in complete darkness.

I then focused on recovering the sensation in my toes, which I hadn't felt for a while. It was a strange sensation to press my toes without feeling them — it had never happened to me before, and I was frightened by the numbness. I started pressing and releasing them, rubbing one foot against the other, and pressing and releasing them again. I felt cold, and to top it off, the wind had intensified. Suddenly, sleet began to fall, quickly turning into large snowflakes descending from the sky. It was as if I were being tested to the limit of my capabilities — I was already without light, without fire, with wind, snow falling, and knowing that I would have to spend the night there.

Survival skills are not only about facing adverse physical conditions; they also involve mental and emotional preparation to endure a prolonged emergency. The ability to make rational decisions under stress, the competence to improvise with limited resources, and the emotional resilience to keep morale high are equally critical aspects.

Even though I wasn't injured, the situation was extremely stressful. Queque had just come through a challenging situation at his company, and now he was losing his plane. But before allowing himself to succumb to despair, he focused on the present moment. He needed to get through that night as best as he could — to survive. There would be time to deal with everything else later. In that difficult moment, it was essential to maintain a balanced mental state to make sound decisions and improve the chances of survival.

He relied on all the techniques he knew. And once he was somewhat settled, he decided first to accept the reality of the situation without denying it, to focus on finding solutions rather than regretting what had happened.

He made an effort to keep a positive and optimistic attitude. He assessed his provisions, knowing he would need to ration them for the next day but also that he needed to keep his body nourished and hydrated.

While trying to improve my temperature conditions and massaging my feet, I began to feel in the darkness that the snow was piling up on me, that weight was accumulating on top of me as if I were being buried. Snow had begun to fall heavily, with enormous flakes descending as if in slow motion. The wind had suddenly calmed, creating a beautiful scene and an almost oppressive silence surrounding the snowfall. Then I remembered that the forecast wasn't favorable for the following day. It called for heavy rain overnight, but due to the elevation and colder temperatures, that rain here in the high mountains meant snow. How could they rescue me then? Even if they managed to find a helicopter, it couldn't fly in these weather conditions. But I couldn't despair. I had to reset my plan; I was increasingly dependent on myself, and I needed to be strong. I had to preserve my physical

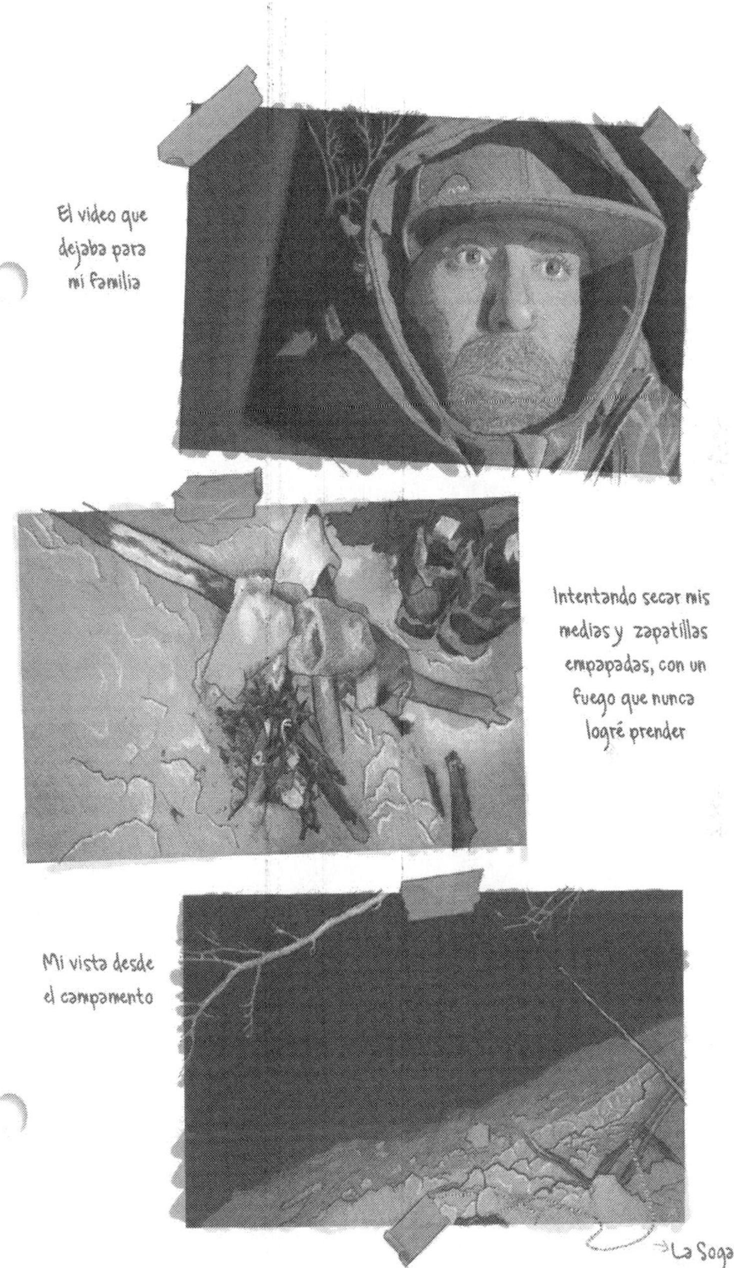
El video que dejaba para mi familia
Intentando secar mis medias y zapatillas empapadas, con un fuego que nunca logré prender
Mi vista desde el campamento
La Soga

strength but, above all, I couldn't lose heart.

In my mind, a thought repeated powerfully whenever I felt uncertain about what I should do: I told myself, "You can't die here; you have to get out of this. It's not just you; your family is waiting for you; your life can't end here." Every time I heard myself saying this, a new idea would come to mind. I spent the entire night thinking about what I would do, and when doubt returned, the same phrase echoed in my head: "You can't die here; you have to get out of this. It's not just you; your life can't end here." At times, I felt the urge to sleep, but I knew that would be very dangerous, almost like surrendering. When that feeling arose, I started massaging my feet, which helped blood circulation and kept me awake and active.

I turned on the flashlight again and realized that the entire orange nylon bag was wet. The condensation from the minimal warmth my body generated, contrasting with the snow covering me, had created moisture inside the nylon bag. Gravity had caused a significant amount of moisture to accumulate in the lower part of the bag, and I began to feel wet and very cold.

The sun set around 6 p.m. and would rise around 9 a.m. I spent all those hours thinking about what the plan should be. In an effort to stay positive, I thought I should add a helicopter to my company's resources so that, if someone else ever had to go through what I was experiencing, we could help prevent them from enduring it.

From my current position, I started imagining how valuable it would be to have such an essential rescue tool stationed in a strategic location like Trevelin—something capable of overcoming geographic obstacles, offering speed, versatility, and the ability to provide medical and logistical support in critical situations.

It could also be used to transport a couple of wildfire

fighters as soon as a fire begins—something crucial in our region. A quick response could prevent thousands of hectares of native forest from burning.

I began exploring possible ways to acquire this tool. I was convinced of its necessity. I would have to find a way to obtain it without relying on any government support. For years, they had neglected the National Gendarmerie's Aviation Section, which had a well-organized structure. They had built a runway, a good hangar, and had qualified personnel on-site. But the aircraft owned by the institution were increasingly grounded due to lack of maintenance and funding. Those still flying were moved from one place to another as needed. I would need to obtain a helicopter through my own efforts, without depending on any government.

These thoughts helped me pass a good portion of the time; they kept me company in a positive way and pushed away any discouraging thoughts.

I went over my plan again. I would wait for the sun to rise, turn the bag, which was currently my first insulating layer, into a first skin by cutting it in half and transforming it into socks and a shirt using the adhesive gauze tape from my first aid kit. This would help retain my body heat and provide some relief from the discomfort of walking with wet socks, pants, and shoes for many hours. I knew the day would be short; I needed to make the most of all the daylight hours to reach Lake Cholila or, as a second option, get out of the snow so I could start a fire. With the last bit of light, I had seen a sort of clearing that seemed to connect Cerro Plataforma with Cerro Tres Picos, but I didn't know how to get there.

While I was thinking, a gust of wind blew the orange nylon bag off me. Fortunately, I managed to trap it against a tree with my left foot. I was forced to turn 180 degrees on the snow, lying in a fetal position. Not even 15 minutes had passed when the same thing happened again; the wind was very strong and constantly shifting. It didn't have a fixed direction, attacking me from various angles. Would it not leave me alone? I tried to prevent too much snow from accumulating on my body to avoid excessive condensation. I pulled my flashlight out of my small shelter, but I couldn't see anything anymore—the snow had covered me beyond the edges of my body. Suddenly, my flashlight ran out of battery, and I was plunged into complete darkness, only able to imagine what was happening around me.

It was a very long night, with hours that felt eternal, and the cold threatened to consume everything. Suddenly, in the middle of the night, I heard a deafening noise very close to me. I knew instantly—an avalanche had broken loose and tumbled down into the valley. But my position was safe. When I was setting up camp with the last bit of daylight, one of the things I was most mindful of was avoiding any potential avalanche paths.

In the morning, as I poked my head out of my improvised shelter, I saw a bit of light, but the clouds covered everything, making visibility very poor, and I feared losing my way. Judging by the slope, I guessed which direction to take toward Cholila and prepared to set off.

I cut the thermal bag I had been using as a base layer, creating a second skin. I admit, I felt a bit guilty, as it belonged to Dany, but at that moment, everything was fair game. There would be time to replace it, and my life was still on the line. I saw it as nearly impossible for an air rescue to be deployed, given the terrible weather conditions. I wrapped the material around my legs, taping it like leggings with adhesive tape from the first-aid kit. This created a garment between my wet, nearly frozen pants, which were stiff as a board—I had to bang them to soften them up. I put the wet socks on over that layer and, finally, with great effort, slipped on my shoes. Dawn was breaking, and I had survived that harsh night. "It's morning; that's something," I had heard that phrase many times and understood what it meant, but for me, it had never been as significant as it was at that moment.

I packed everything I could find into my backpack, dug my helmet out of the snow, which was barely visible, and couldn't recover some things that had been buried by fallen snow and what the wind had blown over. Immediately, I began walking, searching for a way to reach the pass I'd spotted the previous day to reach the edge of Cerro Tres Picos and head through the valley toward Cholila.

I started walking south, looking for a place to cross the mountain. During the night, the amount of snowfall added considerable difficulty and made each step a challenge. I stopped thinking about anything else and focused on a point ahead of me, setting it as a goal to reach. Once I got there, I picked another, and that allowed me to accumulate small victories that motivated me.

But the energy expenditure was immense. I managed to make it about 250 meters south, leaving the cliff behind, and crossing a very dangerous spot. But to continue forward, I would have to climb at least two mountain ridges, each about 50 meters high. My decision, once again, was not to burn all my energy indiscriminately; climbing would only be done if it were unavoidable. That wasn't an option, so I started heading north, looking for a less challenging and less dangerous pass. I approached a slope I would have to cross laterally since it was very steep, but it offered a safer option. That's when I saw the avalanche I'd heard the previous night; I now knew that was a safe way down. The fresh snow there would no longer be a risk.

Snow had been my environment for many years of my life; I had learned to read it, to know where it accumulated, where it packed, when, and how. Snow science courses fascinated me; I'd taken quite a few to learn how to snowboard on mountains outside of ski resorts, where safety relied on analyzing the snowpack and the cohesion of its layers. I knew that the riskiest combination was within the first 24 hours after fresh snowfall on slopes of 38 degrees or more. After making dozens of snow profiles, my eye was somewhat trained to gauge the inclination and identify dangerous slopes from safer ones. This is somewhat similar to mountain flight training with air currents; the only difference is that air, if it doesn't have something to make it visible like smoke, dust, or snowflakes, is invisible, and the reading is done on the slopes.

I thought so many times about how useful it would have been to have one of my snowboards with me to get out of here. But I didn't have it; all I had was an orange nylon bag in my hand and a few things in my backpack that wouldn't help me get out. Before I started walking, I found some rubber gloves in my first-aid kit and decided to put them on to give my hands an insulating layer against contact with the snow. So, wrapping the orange bag over my hands, I punched my fists into the slope and walked sideways, trying to keep my feet as far apart as possible to avoid creating a cut that could trigger an avalanche. I began to move laterally along one of the cliffs to reach the spot where the snow slab had broken off, causing the avalanche during the night. Each step was placed cautiously: first, the tip of my foot, then the sole made a small firm base to step on, and then my fists, wrapped in the nylon bag, dug into the snow above the first step so I could take the next one with my other foot. This took a long time until I reached the avalanche site.

Once I reached the avalanche site, the slope was intimidating. I can't explain how much I missed my snowboard at that moment. I tried to imitate sliding as best as I could with the gear I had. I placed the nylon bag on the ground, sat on it, and lifted my legs to release the brakes. I accelerated quickly; the speed seemed controllable until I tried to stop and, mistakenly, tried to brake too quickly rather than gradually, which made my legs dig into the snow, almost causing me to take a hard fall. I decided to go more slowly, even if it took longer. I made it to the bottom of the avalanche, where the compacted snow was a bit easier to walk on. But now came the worst part: I had to walk uphill. So much snow, so much fatigue, but the phrase in my mind—"You can't die here; you have to get out of this. It's not just you; your life can't end here"—was like an energy boost. Without physical strength, it gave me the willpower I needed to keep moving. I felt that I couldn't stop, even though I was completely spent, yet each step was incredibly difficult. I had no energy. I started eating sugar-filled candies to see if I could gain a bit more strength, but it didn't seem to be enough. The visibility was very low due to the clouds trapped in the valley. I couldn't see where I knew I needed to go, and more than once, I took the wrong path; this left me feeling frustrated.

At times, I would shout, "Is anyone there?" hoping for an answer, but all I heard was the echo of my own voice bouncing off the mountains. The wind had calmed a bit; dropping about 300 feet made the mountain itself provide some shelter. In the silence during the moments of calm, I could clearly hear the panting of my own breath, which spurred me on to get out of there. I tried to check my watch; I didn't know how long I'd been walking and, at the same time, I didn't want to know how much daylight I had left. I was worried that I couldn't see where I was headed and that I kept having to change my route constantly.

At times, I doubted whether I was walking in the right direction, but again, whenever I felt confused and my mind began to edge toward panic, those powerful words would return to ground me. Did I feel fear? Of course, and I believe fear isn't a bad thing. Fear awakens our senses, it sharpens our focus, but I knew I couldn't allow myself to feel panic. Panic paralyzes us, shuts down our senses, and prevents us from making decisions. I couldn't let that happen. I focused on the people I couldn't fail, the ones who would be deeply hurt if I didn't make it out of here.

Would there be a rescue? I knew that Pablo and Dany had seen me, and they would do everything they could to organize a search for me, but the weather was highly unfavorable, and I doubted it would be possible by air. I had seen them heading south, likely to Cholila, as it was too late for them to reach Trevelin. But I knew that in Cholila, where they had lived until recently, they had many acquaintances—seasoned locals, with good communication technology and vehicles. I tried to align my thoughts with theirs. What would their strategy be? What would I do in their place? The first step would be to inform Claudio Lavirgen, an inspector with the Board, to report the situation and activate the search service. I would try to secure a helicopter as close by as possible. We had this information on hand from pilot forums and social media groups, so finding it wouldn't be too difficult. I would call on all my friends who were in a position to help. But the poor weather was against those plans. Perhaps, then, they would organize a ground patrol to search for me. They could cross Lake Cholila by boat and come up along the trail. We would meet along the way, and they would likely bring me dry clothes and food.

We knew each other very well. We had flown together for quite some time, and Pablo worked closely with me in Trevelin on our shared projects. Suddenly, I realized that just as I was putting myself in their minds, they were likely doing the same with mine. They would be predicting each of my steps, my decisions, my approach to this situation, and I was suddenly filled with a deep sense of peace and confidence that I would be rescued—that I wasn't abandoned to my fate. I only had to endure.

What Queque was thinking was almost exactly what we were coordinating. Our shared training and experience led us to act and make decisions that were compatible, in an implicit, almost instinctive understanding. The lost pilot could anticipate, with a certain degree of precision, the actions and decisions the other would take to search for him.

Additionally, mutual trust played a key role in this situation. We both understood that Queque's priority was to conserve energy, remain visible, and follow basic survival protocols, while I had to calculate efficient search routes and use the available resources effectively and efficiently.

A hypothesis about the lost pilot's behavior could trigger a set of actions that made a lot of sense. This operational affinity, which could be described as "thinking in the same way," arose from a sort of cognitive symbiosis that would increase the chances of a successful rescue.

Indeed, just as Queque assumed, with adverse weather conditions for an aerial rescue, Walter Marchand, a local guide, set out at dawn on a ground search, carrying supplies for an initial recovery.

I kept walking. The clouds started to lift; I think at that moment, for the first and only time since I'd started walking, I looked at my watch. It was noon. I'd been walking since 8 a.m. I could see that I had managed to get closer to the pass I had identified to reach the western slope of Cerro Tres Picos. The pass I still had to cross was a steep forest. I slid down on my orange bag again, which I always kept close in case someone was looking for me. I reached Tres Picos after jumping over a stream and climbing a wall of more than two meters of powder snow. I was happy to have achieved the first part of my plan, but I began to feel so tired that I worried I might not make it out of the snowy zone that day. I knew I had about 5 hours left, and I estimated I had between 5 and 9 kilometers to go to reach the first house between my position and Lake Cholila. But I had to do it; I had to get as far as possible.

Suddenly, the silence and the sound of my labored breathing were interrupted by a noise I quickly recognized: Dany's plane, the Cessna 180, flying high in very turbulent air. The snow blowing horizontally off the mountaintops indicated strong winds at altitude. Yet, he was still looking for me.

I felt so proud to see Dany flying in such challenging conditions. I felt his determination to help and get me out of there. I started waving the orange bag to catch his attention. I knew he wouldn't be able to land, but there was a chance he might drop some food or dry clothes from the plane. I waved and waved the bag, but I realized he didn't see me. He didn't tip his wings. We have a synchronized way of communicating with our planes, especially with each other. Not many people know that Dany was my local inspiration to fly the way we do. Ever since I met him, flying that Cessna 180 with such ease and confidence, I wanted to learn from him, and life gifted me with the feeling of having him as family today.

Later, I learned that he had Bernardo Braig as his co-pilot and observer, both of them searching for me, trying to locate me, but they couldn't. They flew over me but didn't tip the wings, didn't circle back to the same spot, nor made the characteristic turn. Why didn't he come back around? Was it so turbulent that his flight was at risk? Suddenly, I felt a physical and emotional slump. I had anxiously awaited help from the sky, but no backpack would fall my way. I felt overwhelmed, sad, and frustrated. From that point on, each step felt harder and harder. The physical exhaustion was taking a serious toll.

Physical training is crucial for facing these conditions. In 2017, I had a severe injury to my left shoulder that marked the end of my career as a snowboarder. After that injury, it was very difficult for me to return to high-performance sports, so I stopped training my body as intensely as I used to. I felt the lack of physical preparation, the fatigue, the lack of energy. I thought about how essential it is to be physically prepared for such intense survival situations. I made a decision to start training again so that if I ever had to face a similar situation, it wouldn't weigh me down as it did now.

I was about 250 meters from entering the forest. This worried me. If Dany came back, he wouldn't see me inside the forest. He hadn't seen me in the clearing I was in, so he'd be even less likely to spot me in the trees. I hesitated for a few seconds, unsure of what to do. I was stopping due to the exhaustion of sinking into the snow up to my waist with each step in this clearing. While I decided what to do, I grabbed the Gatorade bottle that barely had an inch of liquid left, thinking, "If I stay still, this is going to get worse." The cold was hitting fast, and unlike the previous day, I was much wetter and sweaty, with cotton shirts on (the worst thing for these situations). I couldn't stay still for long. I drank less than half of what was left in my bottle, and as I went to put it away, I noticed a little stream a few meters from me. I decided to refill it and keep going toward the forest. I couldn't stay still. I had realized that the winds would prevent Dany from flying to search for and assist me, so I had to get out of the snow to start a fire and dry my clothes.

By this point, I knew I wouldn't make it to Lake Cholila or likely even to one of the few houses between my location and the Tigre River. I approached the stream, bent down to fill my Gatorade bottle with water, and at that moment, the weight of my backpack pushed me forward, causing me to fall into the stream. The amount of energy I expended to avoid falling completely into the water and soaking myself was immense. It was incredibly difficult to pull myself out of that situation with the little strength I had left. I stood up and decided to keep walking toward the forest. I knew now that the only option was to reach a place where there was no snow. I had a long challenge ahead, and if someone came back by air, they wouldn't be able to see me, or, if they saw me and dropped something, it would likely get caught in a tree. It was a moment of intense internal tension, but I knew the worst thing I could do was stay still. Where I was, there was no chance of starting a fire. I had to get out of the snow before I ran out of daylight.

I made all decisions in short time frames. Cold and exhaustion were competing to see which would overcome me first. The temptation to rest, which would mean succumbing to the cold, was intense, and I was growing increasingly uncomfortable as I accepted that I would likely have to spend another night in the snow. Given my fatigue and the distance ahead, it was probable that this night would be even harder than the last. I saw little chance of escaping the snow before the sun set. My focus was on not stopping, so I kept walking toward what seemed like an abyss—a place that, once entered, left no option but to keep walking until I couldn't take another step. This forest in front of me was the next stage, and it was the one that frightened me the most. I felt the presence of panic, but I didn't let it consume me. I repeated to myself once more the phrase that kept me going: "You can't die here; you have to get out of this. It's not just you; your life can't end here."

But this time, as those words echoed in my mind, I heard a sound that made me look up at the sky again. My first thought was, "Dany is coming back; he has to see me this time." It occurred to me to wave the orange bag perpendicular to his approach so there would be more visible orange surface facing the plane. So, I grabbed the bag by its ends and prepared to wave it as soon as I saw him. But the sound was different—it wasn't the classic noise of the Cessna 180's engine. At a lower altitude and almost at the same distance where Dany had passed a few minutes earlier, a beautiful Bell 407 helicopter appeared. I lifted the bag and started waving it from side to side, watching the helicopter from beneath it. I couldn't believe it. Suddenly, the pilot began flashing the landing light on and off. They had seen me... How can I describe what I felt at that moment? A mix of joy, gratitude, and a sense of calm washed over my exhausted body, eliminating every trace of adrenaline. I felt as if I might collapse, that I wouldn't be able to reach the helicopter, even if it landed right next to me.

As the helicopter landed, I understood why Dany had left the airspace. He had moved aside to make room for the helicopter coming behind him. They were surely in communication, and he had gone ahead to assess the visibility, wind conditions, and to see if they could locate me.

Flying over snow-covered mountains is an experience that, while beautiful, requires deep respect for the power of nature. Proper preparation and knowledge of specific survival techniques are essential for any pilot who wishes to navigate these landscapes safely. The story of this experience aims, on one hand, to prepare for the possibility of an emergency as part of any flight plan, and in the event of an emergency, to remember the hardships Queque had to endure and the strategies he used to survive.

Although this story ended in the best possible way, we made several mistakes, which should be noted if we are to learn from this experience.

First, we flew out very late, extremely limited by the short daylight period at this time of year and in these latitudes. In the same situation, but if events had occurred earlier in the day, the chances of a favorable outcome would have been much higher. Queque likely wouldn't have needed to spend the night there.

Second, our flight preparation did not consider an emergency landing as a possible event. To maximize cargo space, all the PA18 pilot's emergency and survival gear was left in the hangar, including communications equipment.

The Cessna 180's survival kit was at my house in Lobos, and I brought it to Trevelin since I was returning to Buenos Aires in that plane. However, since I had flown commercially on my way here, I avoided packing items like the knife, the radio, and tools in the checked luggage to avoid extra fees. Therefore, the kit was incomplete when we threw it to Queque.

Third, we had not established a protocol for emergency situations, which led to some uncertainty. Had Queque headed down to Cholila or to the Turbio River? We made up for this uncertainty by knowing each other well and understanding how we think. Without fully realizing it, there was a certain synchronization between our minds. Due to our pilot training and mountain experience, we had a good sense of what Queque would be thinking and deciding, and he, in turn, could imagine what we were doing for his rescue.

While living in Cholila and doing the flights that Queque now did, my wife, Silvia, knew exactly what to do if something happened to me. Each time the plane took off for La Esperanza, she would report the departure, and upon arrival at the destination, she would report the landing, and the same process was followed for the return. Additionally, having observed that nearby search services were often disorganized, which we had seen in several situations where we contributed the plane for searches, we decided to rely on our own resources. Silvia understood clearly that the first person to contact in an emergency was Luis "Tito" Tagle. Although informal in some respects, we had great trust in him for this purpose. He knew the area well, the trails, was an experienced mountaineer, and was deeply connected to the local community.

Preparing adequately before embarking on a flight over snow-covered mountains is essential to ensure safety and survival in case of an emergency. Pilots of single-engine planes, due to the limitations of their aircraft in terms of power and range, need to be particularly aware of what it means to fly over these inhospitable areas.

And this preparation isn't limited to flight planning and reviewing weather conditions; it also involves carrying the right equipment to face a potentially hostile environment if an emergency landing is required.

While there is a wide variety of survival gear on the market, our experience has helped us determine the most suitable emergency kit for our needs. Since we must always carry it with us, it shouldn't add too much weight; our backpack needs to be light and compact, yet it must include the essentials for handling emergency situations. First and foremost, it's crucial to have communication and signaling equipment, such as a portable VHF aviation radio, a personal locator device or emergency beacon, and possibly a signaling mirror and a whistle.

A few years ago, a group of paragliders called me to help in the search for an adventurer who had attempted to cross from El Bolsón to Cholila and got lost along the way. They had searched for him all day, but the mountains that separate these two places are quite rugged. Since it was too late to set out, I promised to search the area at dawn. Importantly, they mentioned that he had a radio and provided the frequency.

As soon as I entered the area where he was likely located, I began calling for him, and he responded immediately, giving me his physical condition and approximate location. I relayed this information to his companions, who were on standby to set out for him, and they found him in a very short time.

For navigation and orientation, there is plenty of technology available, with the most accessible being a portable GPS. Nowadays, they come in very small sizes, even mounted on a wristwatch. This not only provides the exact location based on coordinates but also helps in cases like Queque's, where he was trapped between clouds and without visibility.

During the winter, it's very possible, as in this case, that an overnight stay at the accident site may be necessary, given the short days. Therefore, it is essential to carry protective and insulating equipment, such as an emergency thermal blanket that reflects body heat and provides an additional layer of protection against the cold, and a sleeping bag that, even if not rated for extreme cold, can withstand low temperatures and be compacted into a small bundle. If possible, add a very thin, lightweight sleeping mat—not for comfort, but to insulate against the damp ground, as direct contact with cold ground can quickly drain body heat. Additionally, bring a light set of thermal clothing—a shirt, pants, and socks, wrapped in a waterproof bag. In such situations, there are few things as comforting as putting on dry clothes and getting into a sleeping bag.

Being able to start a fire is extremely important. Not only does it help prevent hypothermia and dry wet clothes, but it is also highly visible from the air. Rising smoke serves as a perfect indicator of one's position.

To start a fire and maintain warmth, the kit should include at least two lighters, waterproof matches, or an emergency fire starter. But in winter, the entire forest is often very damp, so some type of fire starter material is needed, such as cotton balls soaked in petroleum jelly, fire-starting tablets, or gel fuel. An old Welshman from Trevelin, who enjoyed hunting boars in winter, told me he always carried a piece of car tire in his saddlebag, which allowed him to start a fire anywhere and in any condition. I've tried it a few times, but I feel it's more effective to carry glycerin or other more efficient fire starters.

On this occasion, we couldn't get a camp heater with a gas canister, but now I feel it's essential to bring one in winter. I'd always feared that canisters could explode at altitude, but the truth is they withstand a much higher internal pressure than what altitude could cause. In fact, Alaskan pilots typically include them in their survival kits.

Along with this, a small metal cup is essential—for melting snow or making coffee, tea, or an instant soup to have a hot drink. If you've never had cream of asparagus or pea soup in these conditions, you can't imagine how delicious it feels. Additionally, the kit should contain high-energy foods, such as energy bars, nuts, and chocolate, as well as compact emergency rations. A basic first-aid kit with bandages, antiseptics, essential medications, and small scissors is also necessary.

A multi-tool or survival knife, along with at least 10 meters of thin but strong rope capable of supporting a person in case of a difficult descent or cliff crossing, and a tactical flashlight with charged batteries. Recently, we also added a solar charger for the cell phone, which can also be used to recharge a GPS or other device as needed.

Something that helped a lot in this case was a waterproof plastic sheet in a bright orange color, which contrasts with the landscape and is easy to spot. It should be large enough to use as a shelter cover.

The clothing worn during the flight should also be appropriate. I remember once my father had to fly over the restricted area of Los Alerces National Park at the request of the Park Administration.

As a flight instructor, he would often invite one of his students to accompany him. This time, the available student was a young man from El Bolsón who was embracing the hippie movement, which was very popular there at the time.

The instructor and the student had very distinct and contrasting profiles—the former, a conservative ex-military man, and the latter, displaying his anti-establishment ideology through his appearance and clothing. But fortunately, there was no animosity between them, only a playful provocation. The student, enjoying this dynamic, would notice his instructor's discomfort whenever he showed up with a scruffy appearance, shoulder-length hair, and a small earring. But there was nothing to criticize in terms of his flying skills; despite the instructor's high expectations, the student responded with discipline and proficiency.

But for this flight, he showed up in a tunic and sandals, giving the instructor an opportunity to deliver a lesson in common sense. What if they had an emergency in the mountains? How did he expect to handle himself in the middle of the Valdivian forest dressed like that? He sent the student to change and put on proper shoes, and the student had nothing to argue—because the old man was right.

Appropriate clothing is one of the first lines of defense against the extreme cold often encountered at high altitudes and snowy terrain. It's wise to dress in layers, as this allows for adjustment of insulation levels depending on environmental conditions. A base layer of thermal clothing wicks moisture away from the body, keeping the skin dry. Over this, an insulating layer helps retain body heat, and finally, a wind- and waterproof outer layer provides protection against the elements.

In addition, waterproof jackets and pants are recommended, sturdy enough to endure prolonged exposure to harsh conditions. It's also essential to bring gloves, a warm hat, and a scarf to protect extremities and the head, which are areas prone to rapid heat loss. Insulated boots are also a good measure; they should not only be waterproof but also offer good insulation and traction for walking on slippery surfaces like snow and ice.

Anyone who has watched a series about flying in Alaska and paid attention to the pilots' clothing will have noticed that they are typically prepared for the extreme weather conditions they continuously face. An emergency landing in a mountainous area covered in snow and ice can be a traumatic and disorienting event. However, the initial actions taken after such an event are crucial in setting a path toward survival and rescue. The priority is to stay calm and assess the situation with clarity, enabling the best possible decisions in the circumstances.

Following a certain order, which should be ingrained as a standard response in case of such an incident, the first step is to evaluate the physical condition of the crew for any injuries or impairments that might hinder movement, while also checking for fuel leaks or fire hazards with the aircraft.

Next, assess the immediate surroundings. This includes identifying additional hazards, such as proximity to cliffs, steep slopes, or avalanche-prone areas. If the aircraft is in an unstable position, it's necessary to evacuate safely to avoid further injuries. The priority is to ensure a safe, stable environment to proceed with the next steps.

Afterward, a provisional shelter should be set up. If conditions permit, the aircraft itself can serve as temporary shelter, providing protection from wind and snow. It's important to seal any openings, such as broken doors or windows, with fabric, clothing, or any available material to minimize heat loss.

In addition to serving as a good shelter, the aircraft is far more visible from the air than a person, making it easier for search and rescue teams to locate. Leaving the aircraft could significantly reduce the chances of being found quickly and increase the risks associated with the environment.

In Queque's case, using the plane as a shelter wasn't possible because it was in a dangerous situation—he didn't know the thickness of the ice. Using it for shelter could mean ending up at the bottom of the lake, leading to certain death.

If the plane cannot be used for shelter due to damage or unsafe conditions, a nearby protected spot should be sought for refuge. This could involve finding a natural depression in the terrain that offers protection from the wind or using landscape features such as large trees or rocks as barriers. At this stage, the priority is to minimize exposure to the elements and conserve body heat.

When establishing a shelter, it's essential to consider the risk of avalanches, one of the most significant natural hazards in the mountains. Avalanches occur when a mass of snow and ice breaks loose and slides rapidly down a slope. The unique shape of the mountain makes it particularly prone to these types of events. Snow hanging from cliffs can fall due to melting or, as in this case, due to increased accumulation from snowfall, triggering a surface flow of snow. It could also be triggered by something as simple as walking across a snowy slope.

It's important to recognize avalanche-prone areas. Slopes with angles between 30 and 45 degrees are particularly susceptible. The recent accumulation of fresh snow, especially following a storm, can significantly increase the risk. Warning signs include cracks in the snow, a change in snow texture, or hollow sounds when walking on it.

If an avalanche is suspected to be possible, it is crucial to avoid these areas whenever possible. Stay in areas protected by natural formations like rocks or dense forests that can act as barriers. Additionally, in some cases, digging safety trenches or building shelters that provide some protection in the event of an avalanche may be helpful.

If a snow avalanche begins to form, try to move toward the edges, where the snow's speed and mass are lower. If caught, make swimming motions to try to stay on the surface. Once the movement stops, create an air pocket in front of your face to help with breathing, and if possible, try to signal rescuers with any part of your body that may be outside the snow.

The greatest risk for people is being buried under the snow, which can lead to death or injury from impact, as the force of an avalanche can cause serious or fatal injuries—those in its path may be dragged and hit by descending snow or against rocks, trees, or other structures. Asphyxiation is also a danger, as compacted snow can be as hard as cement, hindering movement and breathing.

Once a safe location is established, building shelters becomes a priority. One such shelter is the quinzee, which is built by piling up snow and then hollowing out a space inside. To construct it, a large amount of snow should be gathered, preferably for at least an hour, allowing it to settle and compact. Then, an inhabitable space is dug into the mound, creating a dome shape to distribute the weight of the snow and prevent collapse. It resembles an igloo, but unlike an igloo, which is made with blocks of hard snow, the quinzee is built by piling loose snow.

Snow caves can also be built. If natural snow formations are found, such as cavities or wind-formed hollows, they can be expanded and adapted as shelters. These natural shelters offer faster construction and generally provide good protection against the wind. From a design and efficiency perspective, it's important that the entrance is close to the ground, allowing cold air to stay below and warm air to remain above.

While the main goal is to retain heat, proper ventilation in the shelter is also essential, especially in closed shelters like a quinzee or snow cave. Lack of ventilation can lead to a dangerous buildup of carbon dioxide, especially if using a heater. It is advisable to create small vents or leave a small opening for fresh air circulation. These vents also help to prevent moisture buildup, which can make the shelter colder and damp.

Once the provisional shelter is established, immediate needs should be prioritized. The pillars for survival in extreme conditions include warmth, water, food, and communication. Warmth is essential to prevent hypothermia. In addition to wearing appropriate clothing and using thermal blankets, light physical exercises can help maintain circulation and generate body heat. Access to water is another critical aspect. If snow is available, it can be melted to obtain drinking water. However, it's important to remember that snow should be melted before consuming to avoid lowering body temperature. Additionally, snow doesn't provide a significant amount of water by volume due to its low density, making it an inefficient hydration source.

Regarding food, although it is not an immediate priority, an inventory of available supplies should be taken, and rationing should begin prudently to avoid weakening. Food provides the necessary energy to maintain bodily functions and morale. It's useful to make an inventory of available food and calculate its potential duration. High-energy foods like granola bars, nuts, chocolate, and dried fruit are preferable as they offer a high amount of calories in small portions.

In some cases, it may be possible to find additional food sources in the environment, such as berries, roots, or even small animals. However, this should be done carefully and with proper knowledge to avoid ingesting poisonous plants or dangerous animals.

In Patagonian lakes and rivers, there is a constant presence of fish. Salmonids are skilled swimmers and capable of reaching high-altitude basins, overcoming rapids and waterfalls. Therefore, including a few meters of fishing line and some hooks in the survival kit can provide access to fresh, high-quality protein. In any area, it's possible to find bait, such as worms, small frogs, horseflies, or some aquatic invertebrates that can be found under rocks.

An often underestimated aspect of the initial actions following an emergency landing is maintaining morale. In extreme situations, the mental state of individuals is crucial for decision-making and the ability to endure until rescue arrives. It's beneficial to establish a routine, even in the first hours, to create a sense of normalcy and control. This can include simple tasks such as organizing the shelter, preparing food rations, and setting schedules for watching for rescue signals.

Keeping busy and focused on specific tasks helps to avoid despair and panic. Additionally, if there is more than one person, it's helpful to assign roles and responsibilities to foster a sense of purpose and cooperation. Open communication and mutual support are essential to maintain a positive attitude and solve problems as they arise.

Once shelter is secured and immediate basic needs are covered, the next step for survival is to maximize the chances of being found by rescue teams. In a snowy mountainous environment, visibility may be limited, and weather conditions can change rapidly, making effective signaling essential.

Visual signals are a way to communicate with aerial and ground rescue teams. It's important to create signals that are easily visible from a considerable distance. Using the snow to form a large "X" or the letters "SOS" with contrasting objects, such as branches, stones, or even dark clothing, can be seen from the air. These signals should be large enough to be visible from high altitudes, ideally with each letter being at least three meters long. Reflective materials, such as signaling mirrors, metallic parts from the aircraft, or even a cell phone screen, can also be used to catch the attention of passing aircraft. During the day, sunlight can reflect off these objects, creating flashes visible from a long distance.

Queque used a large orange plastic sheet, which was very visible against the snow, allowing the helicopter crew to locate him quickly.

However, if flammable material is available, starting a fire is the most effective way to be detected, as smoke can be seen from very far away. Green branches can be kept ready, and if an airplane or helicopter is heard, they can be added to the fire. This will immediately create blue smoke, acting like a large, visible beacon. At night, the fire not only provides warmth but also serves as a visible beacon. During the dry season, it's important to be mindful of fire safety in wooded areas to prevent forest fires.

Queque would occasionally shout, and if he had had a whistle, he would have used it. It is recommended to blow three consecutive blasts, which is an internationally recognized distress signal. Whistles can be heard at greater distances than the human voice and don't require the same physical effort. If a patrol is searching on the ground, these auditory signals could be picked up and become very important if visibility is low due to fog or darkness.

If a firearm for signaling is available, three shots in the air can also be used as a distress signal. It's important to use this resource wisely, as it may be limited, and safety should also be considered.

Electronic Locator Equipment

Personal Locator Beacon (PLB): The PLB is one of the most effective devices for signaling an emergency. When activated, it sends a distress signal that includes the user's exact location, thanks to integrated GPS technology. This signal is received by satellites and then transmitted to rescue authorities, allowing for precise location tracking. It is crucial that the PLB is registered and updated with accurate personal information to facilitate the rescue process.

Use of Flares: If flares are available, they should be used strategically when a nearby aircraft or rescue team is detected. Signal flares are extremely visible, but they usually have a short burn time, so they should be used sparingly to maximize effectiveness.

In some cases, as in the story here, it may be necessary to abandon the aircraft because it's in an unstable situation, because one of the crew members knows of a nearby shelter, or because the rescue team has instructed them to move to an extraction point.

If it is necessary to move from the original site for any reason, a clear message should be left. This can include a written note with information on the direction taken and the reason for leaving, or visual signals indicating the chosen path, such as lines or arrows formed with branches or stones pointing in the direction taken. These notes can be placed in visible locations, such as the aircraft cabin or a weather-resistant metal box.

Managing Physical Activity

Physical activity must be controlled. It should be moderated to avoid exhaustion. Intense activity can lead to a rapid loss of calories and water, as well as increased sweating, which can result in a loss of body heat. Light, periodic exercises are recommended to maintain circulation and warmth, while avoiding excess.

Maintaining energy levels also requires adequate rest. In a survival setting, it's easy to underestimate the importance of rest, but the body needs time to recover. Creating a comfortable space to rest within the shelter, insulated from cold and wind, is beneficial for ensuring proper rest.

Importance of sharing experience

Emergency situations in single-engine aircraft represent critical moments in aviation, where the pilot's skill, knowledge, and preparation are put to the ultimate test.

When a pilot shares their experiences during an emergency, they open a window to a world of learning that would otherwise remain closed. These accounts allow other pilots to understand the real, practical challenges that can arise in flight, beyond the theoretical scenarios taught in classrooms. The experience of a pilot who has faced an engine failure mid-flight, a loss of control, or adverse weather conditions provides firsthand lessons on managing stress, making quick and effective decisions, and applying emergency procedures efficiently.

Moreover, these stories enrich the collective knowledge base, creating a legacy of practical wisdom that transcends generations. Each emergency story brings unique details, specific contexts, and creative solutions that can be adapted and applied in future, similar situations. By documenting and sharing these events, a culture of safety and continuous learning is fostered within aviation, where every incident becomes an opportunity to improve and prevent future accidents.

The importance of recounting emergency situations also lies in humanizing the profession of a pilot. Pilots are not infallible machines; they are human beings who sometimes have to face difficult circumstances. Their survival stories and successes not only inspire their colleagues but also reinforce the importance of rigorous preparation, discipline, and a resilient mindset.

Ultimately, narrating emergency experiences in single-engine aircraft is an act of responsibility and generosity. It is a way to contribute to the well-being and safety of the aviation community, ensuring that every pilot is better equipped to face the unexpected challenges that flight may present. It is a legacy of knowledge and experience that, when shared openly and honestly, saves lives and builds a safer, more prepared future for aviation.

Queque's sincere and detailed account is part of this context, understanding the importance of sharing knowledge gained from real-life experiences, providing invaluable lessons that cannot always be obtained in a controlled training environment. By sharing both his mistakes and successes, he offers his colleagues the opportunity to learn from authentic situations, understanding the consequences of each decision, and helping to prevent the repetition of similar mistakes.

His honesty in recounting his experience strengthens trust within the pilot community, demonstrating that aviation is a field of constant learning where everyone can contribute to growing in safety and continuously improving procedures.

Additionally, Queque confesses that, from a perspective of personal and professional development, sharing these trials allows him to reflect deeply on his actions and decisions, generating a critical self-assessment essential for his own growth.

These survival and emergency management stories are deeply inspiring. They show that, despite mistakes, it is possible to overcome extreme situations with determination and skill. Pilots who share their experiences can become role models, inspiring others to be open and honest about their own experiences.

CHAPTER 3
SEARCH AND RESCUE

Search and rescue operations in the Patagonian mountains are relatively frequent events, given the numerous incidents involving skiers venturing off-piste in winter resorts, hikers losing their way in rugged terrain, climbers in distress, and, in some cases, people trapped by avalanches. In the Patagonian cities close to these adventure and mountain sports locations, there are usually well-organized groups from alpine clubs, military forces, or highly experienced volunteers. These teams have acquired vast experience over the years and are always ready to participate in these operations, driven by a strong sense of solidarity and commitment to the community.

Recoveries in these areas generally follow a meticulous, systematic, and coordinated approach to ensure maximum efficiency and minimize the inherent risks of the operation. From the moment an accident report is received, or an emergency signal is activated, there is a rapid mobilization of rescue teams who mostly operate in relatively nearby areas and have the resources and self-sufficiency required to carry out the tasks without needing to call on other agencies.

However, when the incident involves an aircraft accident, the situation takes on an entirely different scale. Not only does it attract greater media attention, but specific protocols and much more regulated procedures are also activated. In these cases, agencies and organizations specializing in aeronautics are involved, and their actions are subject to strict regulations, raising the level of coordination and complexity of the rescue. These aerial operations, due to their nature and severity, require exceptional precision and care, as well as collaboration among multiple specialized entities to ensure the success of the mission.

The Event

Both planes taxied together toward the threshold of Runway 27 at LZA. We were ahead in the Cessna 180, positioning ourselves at the runway's end behind the Cub, ready to take off next. But Queque, almost showcasing STOL (Short Takeoff and Landing) performance, made a 180-degree turn halfway down the runway and positioned himself facing the lake for an immediate short takeoff.

Taking off to the east with calm winds was also a good option, with a favorable slope and already on the intended heading. We had done it many times to save time, or with a heavily loaded plane, or because the wind came from that direction. However, in these cases, as soon as we start the climb, we encounter a mountain positioned crosswise to the valley, which is impossible to clear, requiring us to enter and follow the twists of a narrow canyon that holds the outlet river and leads to the valley of Lake Puelo, located very low above sea level.

Despite the uphill slope, we have adopted a standard practice of taking off toward the west, as it is generally safer. Once past the landing field, Lake Esperanza opens up in full view, providing ample space for a wide turn and reversing the heading to exit the valley comfortably and safely. Additionally, given that the area is surrounded by mountains, this flat surface over the lake allows for gradual altitude gain, making it easier to clear the surrounding elevations without complications.

We positioned ourselves at the threshold and waited for Queque to take off. Once he did, we followed, making a short left climbing turn, catching up with him, and flying alongside. Our speed was significantly higher, so we took the opportunity to traverse the Turbio River valley up to Cerro Derrumbe, allowing him time to prepare for the crossing over Cerro Plataforma.

Before attempting the mountain crossing, we took the precaution of reorganizing into formation, adjusting the distance between our aircraft to maintain a safe separation. As we approached the mountain, the air began to feel restless and turbulent, as if nature was warning us about what was to come. I decided to gain altitude to better assess the conditions we were facing, ascending to 6,000 feet, where, as expected, the air didn't calm but instead grew more chaotic and intense. Realizing the increasing wind strength, I communicated with Queque to warn him of the stronger winds and turbulence at higher altitudes, fully aware that the PA18, being such a lightweight aircraft, would be particularly vulnerable to these conditions. Its structure, designed for agility and low-speed flying, would become a disadvantage in such circumstances.

As we maintained our formation, we began entering the wide plateau of Cerro Plataforma, where the wind tended to stabilize. Through the radio, we received an "OK" confirmation to proceed safely. From a higher altitude, we watched as the Piper Super Cub began a cautious descent. The small, fragile aircraft, dwarfed by the vast landscape surrounding it, glided slowly toward the vicinity of the frozen lake. From our cabin, the view was both majestic and deceptive; the snow covering the lake's surface looked like a welcoming, soft, and secure carpet. However, we knew it was merely an illusion created by nature, hiding the true dangers lurking beneath that innocent white layer.

While I focused on keeping our aircraft on course, Pablo, my co-pilot and observer, followed every movement of the Super Cub closely. From his position, he could clearly see how the plane contrasted against the snowy landscape, with the setting sun behind it. Through the intercom, he commented on how beautiful the aircraft looked, highlighting the Cub's colors against the dazzling white of the snow. But then, something changed. Pablo's voice, relaxed until that moment, took on a different tone. It was subtle at first, but his concern became evident when he said, "He's descending too much... Why isn't he stopping the descent?" Those words instantly sharpened my focus, and almost without thinking, I banked the wing to try and get a better view of the Piper, which was to my right, outside my direct field of vision.

A series of disturbing events began to unfold before our eyes. The Piper Super Cub, which had been descending with almost meticulous control, now seemed to be pulled by an invisible string guiding it to the ground. From our position, we could see its shadow moving below, across the icy surface, getting closer as if merging with the plane—a clear, unmistakable sign that it was losing altitude and approaching dangerously close to the ground.

The following moments felt like a fragment of elongated time, where we could observe each detail. The small aircraft's wheels, which seconds before had seemed to float gracefully, made contact with the snow, leaving a small trail on the white surface that deepened with each passing moment. The plane braked abruptly, and what happened next was etched in our memories with painful clarity. With a muffled sound that we could only imagine from our position, the plane lost all stability; the nose tilted forward violently, and in an almost acrobatic motion, the Cub flipped over, its nose digging into the snow. The tail arched upward in a perfect arc, flipping the fuselage completely until it finally came to rest, inverted and crushed against the snow.

From our cockpit, we were helpless witnesses to this dramatic scene. A mix of disbelief, shock, anguish, and helplessness overwhelmed us. From our elevated perspective, we could only be spectators, trapped in the painful reality of our inability to act. The landscape that, minutes before, had been serene and beautiful was now a desolate scene, a silent witness to the misfortune unfolding before our eyes. The whiteness, which had seemed so pure and safe, was now a cruel reminder of the fragile line between the joy of flying and disaster in the mountains.

With my mind tangled in thoughts and emotions but driven by the need to do something despite our limitations, I used the wing's bank and increased pressure on the right rudder pedal to initiate a quick turn, aiming to head directly toward the accident site. While performing the maneuver, we called the Super Cub pilot over the radio, hoping for any response. Our unease grew with each passing second without hearing a reply. As I was at the controls, Pablo urged me to stay focused. We were still in flight, and we needed to maintain stability in our aircraft.

The impact had been violent, and although we knew the lake ice was thick and resilient after months of freezing, we had no way of knowing if it could bear the weight and impact of the plane without giving way. Despite the shock, we tried to stay calm and assess the situation clearly, discussing possible actions to take.

The wait was agonizing. We called out several times, each attempt at communication seeming to increase the despair. Finally, after what felt like an eternity, we heard his voice, firm and determined but pressured by the circumstances. He told us he was okay and that he was leaving the plane out of fear that the ice would break, leading him into an even more dangerous situation.

We began an orbiting pattern, watching as he slowly walked toward the shore, looking for a safe spot. At the same time, we started preparing the survival gear backpack that I always kept on board. However, on this occasion, when I needed it most, what I had previously considered dead weight I merely carried from one place to another turned out to be incomplete.

I had traveled from Buenos Aires to Trevelin to retrieve the Cessna 180, which had been stored there since the summer. My survival kit was with me and had to travel as checked baggage on the airline flight. To avoid the additional cost, I decided to remove some tools, the knife, the radio, and other essential items that I now regretted not having at hand.

I knew Queque had left his own survival gear outside his plane to carry more cargo. Therefore, anything we could drop from the air would be of great use to him. The backpack contained basic items for starting a fire, a sleeping bag, and other things that would help him survive the night in the mountains.

Once he reached the shore, we prepared for a low pass at a slow speed, intending to drop the backpack. Pablo opened the airplane window, releasing the latch that kept it secure to open it completely. The window was wide enough to allow us to throw out large packages, and we had previously dropped supplies in snowy terrain on other occasions.

Queque watched the backpack fall, recognizing it immediately and knowing what it contained. He approached quickly, picked it up, and signaled to confirm he had it.

Rescue Organization

Organizing and executing a mountain rescue is no easy task and demands a constant balance between speed and caution. Every minute counts, but each decision must be made with the highest degree of responsibility, awareness, and efficient resource deployment.

While flying, we used the time to evaluate and inventory our options. Our greatest asset was our network of contacts, with numerous phone numbers of our friends and Queque's friends. Then there was our knowledge of the terrain. We had lived in that area for many years and knew the distances, difficulties, paths, and nearby residents well. We also had access to material and human resources we could obtain from Cholila.

The main challenges were the extreme cold typical of this time in Patagonia—the harshest part of winter, which the pilot to be rescued would have to endure—and the unknowns about whether he had any injuries. Additionally, the forecast indicated unfavorable weather conditions for the mission. In fact, we had flown that day because it was the only one in the week we could do so.

But even if the conditions were marginal, our priority was to find a helicopter and a crew willing to undertake the mission. At the same time, we needed to organize a ground patrol. There was a road that led relatively close to the mountain, although it would likely be obstructed by snow. A boat could also be used to cross Lake Cholila, saving eleven kilometers. From there, we could continue with horses, carrying dry clothes, supplies for a strong fire, and food. We also had a stretcher left at the hangar.

Given the very limited daylight left, we immediately headed toward El Bolsón, intending to start the rescue operation and complete the missing items for the survival kit to drop them in another flyover. Meanwhile, Pablo began making several calls, starting with Claudio Lavirgen, an investigator from the Transportation Safety Board. We knew Claudio, a former Air Force pilot with extensive experience, and very efficient in these situations, aware that he knew how to activate the complex official response system. We also tried calling some people in El Bolsón to prepare the missing items for us. However, the phone service provider we contracted in Buenos Aires proved unreliable in Patagonia, and we couldn't reach everyone until we were practically flying over the city.

As we aligned for the final approach toward Runway 36, we were met with a not-so-surprising sight: the runway was crowded with people, leaving not a single clear space for landing. The situation forced us to make a quick decision; with no other option, although somewhat driven by frustration and pressed for time, we performed a low pass, low enough to unsettle—or at least disturb—the people below and compel them to clear the runway. However, this cost us precious minutes, so we decided to realign and approach from

Runway 18 instead.

The tension was intense, and as we taxied down the runway toward the hangar, we exchanged several insults with those who were still on the runway, who not only shouted at us but also made threatening gestures, clearly upset about our maneuver. Despite the commotion, we managed to reach the southern end of the taxiway, knowing that someone from the aeroclub would come as soon as they heard the engine.

We weren't wrong. As soon as we stopped, we saw Horacio Azcona approaching quickly on his bicycle. After explaining the situation in detail, we asked him to get us a small gas canister with a heater. We knew that in the high mountains, fire was not just a useful resource but a vital necessity, guaranteeing survival in those extreme conditions. Meanwhile, taking advantage of El Bolsón's proximity to the city, I ran to buy chocolate, granola bars, candy, lighters, and both sugary and mineralized water. I explained the situation to the person helping me, who packed everything in a box suitable for a new drop.

I returned to the airfield, but the request for the canister was taking too long, and we didn't have enough daylight left. So, despite the cold and in a somewhat coercive move, I asked Horacio for his jacket, and we tied ours around the box of supplies with a rope to drop it to Queque as reinforcement.

We took off again, and during the flight, one of our major mistakes became evident. We didn't have a pen to write him a note, to tell him we were looking for a helicopter, that we would rescue him no matter what, and to indicate the best path, as we knew the area well. In my flight bag, which holds the plane's documents, I always carry more than one, but that bag was another of the "superfluous" things we had left at our departure point, for a short uncontrolled flight.

When we arrived at the accident site, we noticed he had walked quite a distance, which reassured us as it indicated he was in good physical condition, but his direction was wrong. He had headed directly south, where the cliffs were steep; the exit was to the north, down to the valley, and then toward Cholila.

We dropped this second package with fair accuracy, ensuring it landed where Queque could easily retrieve it, and stayed nearby until we had visual confirmation he had received it. Once we saw him pick up the package and signal to us, we felt a slight sense of relief, though our concern remained. Darkness was rapidly descending over the mountainous landscape, and we couldn't help but express our fear that, in the twilight and rough terrain, Queque might slip off a cliff or suffer an accident. However, we knew he wasn't an amateur but an experienced mountaineer, a snowboarding instructor, and knowledgeable about snow and its dangers. We had to trust in his skill and his ability to navigate the adverse conditions he would face that night.

Aware that time was against us and that nightfall was imminent, we set course for the place that had been our home for so many years, a place we had not only owned but built with great effort. There, we had built our house, prepared an airstrip, and erected a hangar at one end, forming a small refuge in the midst of the wild landscape that would now become the operations center for our rescue mission.

We knew that from there we could organize the search with the efficiency and convenience needed. We had a reliable internet connection, which would allow us to coordinate communications without issues. Additionally, we knew the local people, those who had been our colleagues until recently. We knew their worth, their unwavering willingness to help, and their deep knowledge of the terrain—expert guides, men accustomed to the region's harshness—

and their assistance would be invaluable in a situation like this.

And we not only had trusted people but also material resources that would be very useful for this mission. We had off-road vehicles, a boat to cross the lake, horses for the most inaccessible trails, and a place where we could stay, eat, work, and communicate without distractions.

The next step was to form the rescue teams and then plan the operation, ensuring the teams' safety and establishing a contingency strategy to cover any potential changes or unforeseen events that might arise during the mission. This included an inventory of available resources, communication equipment, and coordination with other services, such as medical assistance.

The first option, hindered by bad weather, was aerial search, rescue, and evacuation via helicopter, as it was the fastest and would allow us to take him directly to a medical facility if his health was deteriorated.

The option of ground evacuation, given the circumstances, was especially considered, for which we would need people accustomed to that type of terrain and strong enough to carry a person on a stretcher over a great distance.

Upon landing in Cholila, we didn't have to wait long before our colleagues, Walter Marchand and Martín Mol, sprang into action. Both, with their characteristic determination, immediately volunteered to help, understanding the urgency and severity of the situation. Without wasting time, we began making the first phone calls, informing the authorities and coordinating the necessary actions to carry out the rescue operation. Every detail, every decision, was crucial to ensuring Queque was brought back safe and sound. And so, in the growing darkness of the night, we embarked on a race against time, driven by the hope that our quick response would positively impact our friend's chances of survival.

We knew that search and rescue operations follow established protocols, requiring the coordination of multiple agencies and the use of resources and technology. Rescuing an aircraft that has crashed in a mountainous area involves not only mobilizing tools and trained personnel but also having a deep understanding of the terrain, weather conditions, and human physiology in extreme cases.

In an ideal scenario, once this phase is declared, all available resources are mobilized for search and rescue. This includes the immediate deployment of search aircraft, helicopters, boats, and specialized ground teams, directed to the last known position of the aircraft or areas where an accident is suspected to have occurred. If the aircraft is on an international route or near the border, coordination with other countries' rescue services expands the search area.

Satellite imagery and advanced detection technologies, such as radar and infrared equipment, are used, especially in remote or difficult-to-access areas, to locate the aircraft as quickly as possible. Meanwhile, Rescue Coordination Centers (RCCs) maintain constant communication, rapidly processing any new information to adjust the search strategy as needed.

Once the aircraft is located, rescue teams move to the site to assist survivors, provide medical care, and arrange for evacuation if necessary. If fatalities are confirmed, the recovery process begins, and the area is secured for a subsequent investigation.

But we were in Argentina, in the distant mountain range of remote Patagonia, and past experiences with heavy snowfalls, floods, forest fires, and even lost persons in the mountains had shown us that the capacity and speed of response would likely not be well-suited to this situation.

Our friend and colleague was in grave danger, and we had

to resolve everything quickly. We relied on our own capabilities and those of our friends, our knowledge of the area, resources, training, and experience for a more immediate rescue. At the very least, we would try to buy time until the services were organized. We made sure to send the alert, confirming that the emergency had already been declared.

It's remarkable how, in crises like the one we were facing, memories accumulated over a lifetime of similar situations resurface involuntarily. It's as if the mind, operating autonomously, tries on its own to contribute to solving a complex situation, weaving together a network of past experiences—be it a memorable flight, adverse conditions, or even the echo of wise advice shared by mentors and colleagues.

In moments of tension, past learnings emerge strongly, like a resource to help evaluate the situation with greater clarity and objectivity for better decision-making. The memory of a successful rescue can give us the confidence needed to face the unknown, while lessons learned from past failures guide us toward a more cautious approach. Thus, every memory and every experience becomes a valuable tool that, collectively, contributes to solving the problem, underscoring the importance of collective experience in overcoming obstacles and safeguarding lives. Ultimately, it is at the intersection of memory and action where the most effective responses are forged.

Emergency Phases

"Lima Víctor Lima Lima Tango, do you read me? Esquel tower is calling!" The voice over the speaker was insistent, indicating they had been trying to reach us for a while.

"Go ahead, Esquel, this is Lima Lima Tango. I'm receiving you weakly. I'll get closer and call again," I replied, adjusting the microphone's position.

"OK. Standing by," the voice on the other end confirmed.

Ten minutes later, I reestablished contact, informing my position and altitude. Estimating was more difficult because with changing wind speeds, I couldn't calculate my true airspeed. But the Piper Cherokee 140 was practically new, equipped with an excellent radio, and although we were still far away, I hoped it would transmit clearly.

"Do you have fuel?" I then recognized my father's voice. It was unusual for him to take control in the tower; the controller probably hadn't arrived, and he'd had to step in. As the airport chief, it wasn't uncommon for him to take on multiple roles in the absence of personnel; he would act as driver, mechanic in the power plant, or tower operator. His question quickly made me realize the reason for his intervention.

I had departed from Trelew with two friends, Ope Williams and David Krieger. I was only 18, and although I had obtained my pilot's license the previous year, I had flown the Esquel-Trelew-Esquel leg several times. It was relatively straightforward, with the high-voltage power line serving as a clear visual guide from the Futaleufú dam to the Aluar plant in Madryn. At the "Bajo de la Tierra Colorada," the line veered slightly north, with Trelew visibly nearby.

We typically estimated two hours for the outbound flight and three hours for the return, due to the prevailing west wind. I had planned the flight based on this information, with an endurance of four hours and fifteen minutes. I hadn't been able to fully refuel the tanks because I didn't have enough money to do so.

The navigation was proceeding as planned until, while crossing the Chubut River, the plane seemed to stop in midair. The river and the small hill known as Gorro Frigio, a reliable landmark for both legs of the journey, appeared stalled. I experimented with different altitudes until the Cherokee suddenly began to move more smoothly. However, my estimated time to the destination airport was completely disrupted.

My companions, who were not familiar with aviation at that time and as young as I was, had no idea of the situation that was unfolding—the serious question of whether I would have enough fuel to make it. But I chose not to convey my concern.

A storm of options raged in my head. I considered diverting slightly south to fly over the dirt road that passes near Arroyo Pescado, closer to the high-voltage line, but that detour would almost certainly mean not making it. I thought about completely emptying one tank but decided it would be wiser to keep a small reserve for a more controlled emergency landing if necessary. Esquel Lagoon, about fifteen kilometers from the airport, offered a viable space for such a contingency. I switched tanks, selecting the one that seemed to have the most fuel.

I was now over Gualjaina Creek, in a well-known area, and although it didn't change my situation, it gave me a sense of security. In the distance, I spotted Cerro Nahuelpán, with its distinctive and recognizable profile. The airport lay before it, and before that, Esquel Lagoon, which presented several flat areas for an emergency.

My fuel indicators on the panel showed critical levels, but the final decision would be made over Cerro Roberts, a moderate elevation that crosses the route and is known for downdrafts that would require maximum power to clear.

Suddenly, the wind dropped significantly, and the ground began to move by faster. The dreaded mountain became nothing more than a beautiful landscape, and after four hours and fifteen minutes of flight, we touched down on the runway and taxied to the hangar. The controller, airport chief, flight instructor, and father of the pilot—all those roles of authority over me—appeared at the hangar and didn't hold back on delivering a powerful scolding in front of my friends. Immediately afterward, he opened the fuel tanks and showed me they were empty. During the taxi, I had switched tanks again, fearing the engine might stop in the middle of the runway, thus depleting the remaining fuel.

"You were in INCERFA!" he reprimanded me. I wasn't yet familiar with the term and didn't know what it meant. However, the situation was clear: my father was certain I had miscalculated the ETA, and to avoid the additional complications of escalating to an emergency declaration, he had taken responsibility. Fortunately, I made radio contact, which reassured those awaiting our arrival.

The meteorologist assured me that I had flown into a "jet stream"—a phenomenon that rarely occurs at those levels—a sort of Venturi effect between two air masses that accelerates the flow. In hindsight, I don't think that was the case, but it certainly lessened my lack of foresight. I then understood that on any journey: Always have full tanks!

On the other hand, I learned from that experience—though I should have known this beforehand—that if an aircraft fails to communicate with air traffic controllers (ATC) or the control tower at the expected time, a series of actions are triggered to reestablish contact. At that time, only radio frequencies were available, and attempts would be made to contact other aircraft in the area to establish communication with the lost plane. Nowadays, more communication tools are available.

If these communication attempts fail and the aircraft does not reach its destination on time, the situation is assessed by reviewing the planned flight route, the last known position of the aircraft, the fuel on board, weather conditions, and any other relevant information. Flight plans are checked, and contact is made with the operator of the aircraft, such as the airline or the owner in the case of a private flight, to gather more details.

When this happens, a series of standardized procedures are initiated to trigger a search and rescue operation, following international protocols established by the International Civil Aviation Organization (ICAO) and adapted by the civil aviation authorities in each country.

At the same time, emergency phases are considered—standardized procedures that guide the response of search and rescue services when it is suspected that an aircraft may be in danger. These phases, defined by ICAO, are used worldwide to coordinate responses in emergency situations.

The first is the Uncertainty Phase (INCERFA), followed by the Alert Phase (ALERFA), and finally the Distress Phase (DESTREFA), where the emergency is declared, and search protocols are activated.

From EANA SE (Argentine Air Navigation Company), which provides public air navigation services, it is mandated that whenever a pilot lands at an uncontrolled aerodrome or declared runway after flying in controlled airspace, they must notify their landing to the relevant air traffic service as soon as possible. Otherwise, the uncertainty, alert, and emergency phases will be followed, and search services will be triggered.

The issue arises in many places in our country where communication is difficult, and it's hard for some controllers to understand this. Some allow the flight plan to be closed before breaking the radio link, but they rarely accept "I will not report arrival," a term previously used as a resource for such cases, so an alternative form of notification must be sought.

Furthermore, they become quite strict about the lack of arrival notification, stating that it is a violation of the Argentine Civil

Aviation Regulations (RAAC) and constitutes an offense subject to penalty, as outlined in Article 2, which states: "A warning, fine, or temporary suspension of up to six (6) months will be applied to holders of certification for exercising aeronautical functions, and a warning or fine for other aeronautical activities. The fine shall not exceed twenty-five percent (25%) of the amount resulting according to the provisions of Article 1, paragraph 2, subparagraph (a) or (b)."

They determine that, in the absence of arrival notification to the respective air traffic control unit, the alert service and emergency phases will be activated, mobilizing the corresponding resources and logistics according to the information detailed in the flight plan. Therefore, any modification that affects the estimated arrival time provided to the ATC must always be communicated before the scheduled end time. Failure to do so may lead to the activation of these services.

However, in the case of general aviation, especially small aircraft that use many LADs (Declared Suitable Places) or uncontrolled aerodromes, it is rare for this mechanism to be activated unless there is certain confirmation of an accident. Forgetfulness and lack of cell signal are the main reasons for the failure to communicate arrival. Generally, the nearest police unit is contacted, which then goes to the location to verify that the plane has indeed landed, or a few phone calls to close contacts, the aircraft operator, or family members are sufficient to resolve the situation.

If there is an air traffic control service at the arrival aerodrome, it is easy to report arrival in person, but if not, the pilot has 30 minutes after the estimated arrival time to notify the landing by some means. There is also the option to do so from the air, five minutes before landing, if it is known that no communication means are available in the arrival area. We frequently did this in Cholila and Esperanza when we encountered such issues.

However, regarding this information published by EANA on its website, many pilots question it, arguing that linking arrival notification directly to operational safety isn't feasible and that any pilot headed to an uncontrolled airport or LAD has the option, for a valid reason, not to report arrival, as long as they notify the control unit that they have decided to cancel their flight plan and won't notify arrival.

Aside from interpretations, RAAC 91 on Flight Plan Closure states the following in subsection (n):

"Flight Plan Closure:

1- Unless otherwise prescribed by the Aeronautical Authority, arrival notification shall be made, in person, by radiotelephony, or by data link, as soon as possible after landing, to the relevant ATS unit at the arrival aerodrome, for any flight for which a flight plan has been filed for the entire flight or the remaining portion of the flight to the destination aerodrome.

2- When a Flight Plan has been filed for only part of the flight, distinct from the remaining part of the flight to the destination point, it shall be closed, when necessary, by an appropriate report to the relevant Air Traffic Services unit, as follows:

(i) When a pilot proceeds to close a Flight Plan, they shall inform the relevant Air Traffic Services unit with the phrase "TERMINATING MY FLIGHT PLAN AND WILL NOT REPORT ARRIVAL," in which case no Alert Service shall be provided, as stipulated in subsection (b) of paragraph 91.153 of Part 91 of the RAAC.

Note: Cases in which regulations require the Flight Plan to remain active until the destination point, such as when flying in the Air Defense Identification Zone (ADIZ) or in Controlled Airspace, are excluded".

The Search and Rescue Service (SAR) in aviation is a system

that coordinates a set of air, land, or maritime resources and operations aimed at locating, assisting, and rescuing individuals involved in aeronautical incidents, accidents, or missing aircraft.

The term SAR comes from "Search and Rescue," which has been internationally adopted for its accuracy in describing this type of activity in different settings.

In most countries, SAR is part of a legal framework requiring states to maintain and operate search and rescue services within their jurisdictions, in compliance with international regulations such as those established by ICAO.

Although not a single entity, in many countries, SAR operations are coordinated by a state agency, such as the air force, coast guard, or civil aviation authority, but may involve collaboration among various ministries and agencies to cover airspace as well as land and maritime areas. It is an integrated system that can include multiple government entities and, in some cases, private organizations.

SAR is not a new system, though it has been refined over time with greater knowledge, organizational development, and technological advancements. Its origins trace back to the early 20th century, arising from the need to establish an organized procedure for responding to emergencies as aviation and maritime activities began to grow, addressing the increasing risks faced by aviation pioneers and mariners.

Then came the wars. During World War I, the rapid expansion of military aviation revealed how vulnerable crews were when their planes went down in unexplored regions or at sea, leading to improvised rescue efforts often organized by the military units themselves or by local communities.

After World War II, the accumulated experience during

the conflict—especially in mass rescue operations for aviators and sailors—highlighted the urgency of establishing an organized and standardized international service. This impetus led to the creation of the International Civil Aviation Organization (ICAO), whose initial mission included coordinating efforts to develop a global SAR system, requiring states to establish search and rescue services within their respective jurisdictions, representing a crucial step forward in international cooperation.

My first encounter with this service was many years ago, from a telegraph message received at the Esquel tower.

"Message for aerodrome chief SM Roy Wegrzyn from Captain Juan Carlos García. Tomorrow, stopover at ESQ. Arrange lunch for crew T87 and VIP PAX Comodoro (R) Carnaghi."

Not so many years ago, there was a fairly rudimentary communication system between Patagonian airports for relaying flight information, aircraft arrivals and departures, weather conditions, and more. From today's technological perspective, it was highly inadequate. This information was transmitted via radio, where the operator would clearly interpret about half of it, and the rest was practically guessed. You needed a well-trained ear to communicate. In addition, the tower operators had an extra tool: Morse code, and most were experts in receiving and transmitting data. Messages were sent and received in the form of brief, formal telegraphic notes.

Captain García was one of the pilots and instructors of the Twin Otter planes that the Argentine Air Force stationed at the IX Air Brigade, flying LADE routes throughout Patagonia. He was my father's best friend in the Air Force, and on every stopover in Esquel, he'd have lunch with us while the plane refueled before continuing on to Comodoro Rivadavia. Whenever he had the chance, he'd come with his wife to spend a few days fishing and hunting.

He was one of the pilots who frequently flew to the Malvinas Islands, supporting the islanders. Before the outbreak of the South Atlantic War in 1982, life in the islands largely depended on connections with mainland Argentina, and a key element of this relationship was the State Airline (LADE). This state airline played an important role in maintaining daily life in the islands, facilitating the transport of people and goods between the remote islands and Argentine cities.

LADE's regular flights not only connected the islanders with the rest of Argentina, but they were also essential for supplying a variety of vital resources. Since many of the islands' needs couldn't be met locally, residents depended on these flights for food products, construction materials, equipment, and other essential goods for daily operations and community upkeep.

These trips to the Malvinas allowed Juan Carlos to purchase high-quality fishing equipment, from which we also benefited. Our trout fishing rods and reels were top brands, hard to come by in Argentina at the time.

The plane had just left Bariloche, and my mother, accustomed to these visits and last-minute lunch plans, drew on her creativity, making her well-known pies, empanadas, and pizzas on homemade bread dough. Her cooking had gained fame throughout the IX Brigade, to the point where many pilots found an excuse to extend their Esquel layovers at midday.

The only passengers mentioned in the message were the military governor of Santa Cruz at the time and his wife. My mother asked me to monitor the flight closely so she could prepare lunch in time. So, I went up to the tower. There were only five families at the airport, and we shared a wholesome coexistence. We had a chessboard, and I spent a lot of time engrossed in intense matches with the controllers, who had plenty of time between meteor reports and the occasional flight.

The Twin Otter made a stop in El Maitén and continued to El Bolsón, a 15-minute flight, but the arrival didn't happen. Being in the tower allowed me to witness the initial moments of anxiety when the emergency was declared, and the search and rescue service was activated. My dad was notified through internal communication while he was in his office downstairs. He immediately asked me to come down and help prepare the Cherokee 140 and the C182. Soon after, a notification came from SAR to mobilize all available aircraft and qualified pilots for the search, coordinated by this agency.

Each plane was assigned a zone, and among several Argentine Air Force aircraft, we set out to search. My father requested that special attention be paid to a small hill in the valley between El Maitén and El Bolsón. In conditions of heavy cloud cover, it became very dangerous, and he had pointed it out to me several times.

Simultaneously, hospitals in El Bolsón, El Maitén, and Esquel were alerted to be ready. Well-equipped rescue teams prepared for a possible ground search, including Carlo Botazzi, a mountain expert leading a rescue team for climbers in Bariloche. Ambulances and an air ambulance were also on standby. As a novice pilot, and even in the bitter context of a situation where someone so close was the main object of the search, I was struck by the professionalism displayed by the SAR, then led by the Argentine Air Force, the allocation of resources, and the orderly coordination. Some said it was because the aircraft and personnel involved belonged to the Force, but in a way, this was disproved by the fact that they extended the call to other forces and civilian groups, not only to pilots but also to mountaineers, medical personnel, and local guides.

That first day was fruitless; most of the search was hindered by low visibility. On the second day, they searched all day with no results. The same happened on the third day, even with an expanded search area and additional aircraft from local aeroclubs and other Air Force units from other regions joining in.

The situation became quite desperate, as time is crucial in an aviation accident where there could be survivors. I remember that they didn't even disregard the information provided by some psychics who marked the possible location on a flight chart.

Finally, on the fifth day, an Air Force C130 Hercules located the plane on Cerro Paleta, just above the timberline, where the forest ends and the rocky strata begin. They radioed the discovery and clearly described its condition: "The aircraft is 100% destroyed, no chance of survival."

The reconstruction of events made it evident that the Twin Otter was trapped in low clouds and began a desperate blind spiral climb through the valley. It was about to break free when, likely on the last turn, the mountain obstructed its path. A GPS with a rudimentary screen could have saved it, but unfortunately, these arrived too late for this crew.

The flight attendant, a young man named Laso, with whom we had a friendly relationship, managed to exit the impacted plane and was found dead close to the crash site. The others were found inside the plane.

This was a traumatic experience for a young pilot, introducing me to the world of aviation, which, while filled with wonderful moments, was also touched by these tragic events.

Today, globally, SAR is a highly specialized service involving the coordination of multiple agencies and organizations, both civilian and military. Rescue operations are managed by Rescue Coordination Centers (RCC), which oversee and direct efforts in specific areas. The current approach now includes not only air and sea rescues but also operations in remote and mountainous regions as well as in natural disasters. International cooperation remains vital, with agreements allowing nations to share resources and expertise during crises.

However, while all of this is well-defined on paper, Argentina has suffered a long and severe decline in attention and resources dedicated to aviation, which has led to setbacks in both the quality and quantity of resources and trained personnel once provided by the Argentine Air Force. That dedication and efficiency displayed during the search for the missing Twin Otter in the mountains, despite a lack of advanced technology, is rarely seen today.

Adherence to Protocols

After our landing in Cholila, while we focused on organizing the rescue planned for the following day, we received a flood of calls. Some were from friends offering their unconditional help; others were from media outlets eager for information. However, many were from people identifying themselves as officials from various agencies, demanding that we provide details or submit to various "protocols" before proceeding with any action.

With the cold seeping into our bones, combined with the stress and profound concern for the life of our colleague and friend, who was facing severe weather conditions at a high altitude, without food, water, shelter, and possibly injured, our only thought was the urgent need for immediate action. The idea of not acting to comply with rigid, bureaucratic protocol that would only cause significant delays seemed absurd to us.

This is not, by any means, a call to disregard or neglect established protocols, which are and will remain fundamental pillars for ensuring safety and efficiency in aviation operations. However, it is imperative to recognize that protocols, like any regulatory tool, must be dynamic and adjust to the specific circumstances in which they are applied. Excessive rigidity in their interpretation or implementation can, in certain cases, hinder quick and sound decision-making, especially in environments where variables change rapidly, and adaptability is essential to avoid critical situations.

The need for a clear and well-structured regulatory framework is unquestionable; it forms the foundation upon which operational safety rests. Organizing actions provides predictability and control, two vital factors for mitigating risks. However, it is equally true that, in some contexts, that very structure can become a barrier if it is not considered with sufficient flexibility. Procedures designed to guide and support actions may, at times, slow response capacity or limit the ability to apply professional judgment in situations where adaptability and prompt action are essential.

The intention here is not to question the necessity of procedures but rather to advocate for their constant review to ensure they do not become an unnecessary obstacle. In many cases, excessive bureaucratization or the imposition of overly strict norms overlooks the specifics of the operational environment or the unique context of a situation. It is essential that regulations not only align with global standards but also allow room for maneuvering so that the pilot or rescuer can act effectively and safely, without feeling bound by rigid plans that, though well-intentioned, may prove counterproductive.

It is also important to understand that flexibility in the application of procedures does not imply, in any way, a relaxation of safety standards, but rather an optimization so that they serve their primary purpose: achieving a rescue by facilitating safe operations in an ever-changing environment. Pilots, as trained professionals, must have the confidence and regulatory support to make decisions based on their experience and the specific knowledge of the moment, without feeling stifled by a regulatory framework that, instead of supporting, hinders their work.

In essence, the goal is to evolve protocols toward a more

intelligent, adaptive, and flexible approach, allowing those at the forefront of operations to act with the best judgment, supported by procedures that adapt to operational realities without becoming insurmountable barriers in critical moments.

In this accident, we were directly involved, and our hindsight perception is that if we had relied solely on official agencies, Queque might not have survived. In popular belief, there is trust that emergency teams for these cases are always ready, like town firefighters who spring into action within minutes when the siren sounds, or like ambulances or police, prepared to respond quickly. However, in situations like this, we confirmed that the response is rarely immediate.

Strict protocols often leave little room for rescue coordinators to make quick decisions based on their knowledge and experience. This is especially problematic in high-mountain operations, where conditions can change drastically in an instant, demanding extremely agile adaptability and response.

And although I may judge harshly and from a subjective perspective motivated by anger, I feel that the calls we received took me back to our experiences fighting forest fires, where many of these "protocols" seemed to serve those seeking protagonism, those wishing to shield themselves from responsibility when making decisions, or simply those exercising their authority from positions attained not by merit but through political appointments. Meanwhile, the fire continued to spread, indifferent to procedural, political, or jurisdictional considerations.

I feel a sense of pain and frustration in expressing this, as it reminds me of my father, who lived in a different Argentina in his youth, and whose concern grew as he observed how inept governments took control of the country, effectively dismantling from its foundations what great leaders had built with a vision for the future, patriotism, and a collective spirit. They understood the importance of working for the common good, recognizing that a dignified and prosperous Nation must transcend personal interests.

The inability of those who assumed power to honor and protect that legacy is not only painful; it represents a betrayal of the ideals that defined our homeland. The systematic erosion of our institutions and the loss of fundamental values have created a sense of helplessness and disillusionment that resonates across current generations. This dismantling is not merely a political issue; it is a deep wound that cuts through the very fabric of our identity as Argentinians.

Many of us feel that there is a widespread institutional crisis in Argentina, marked by a deep erosion of the capacity and efficiency of those leading state institutions, exacerbated by the politicization of public administration. Instead of functioning as independent and effective bodies, these institutions are excessively subordinated to political and partisan interests, creating an environment where key decisions are made with a bias that may stem from ineptitude or electoral aims rather than technical criteria or efficiency. This phenomenon is evident at all levels: national, provincial, and municipal.

And although, as I write this, there are faint winds of change bringing hope, politicization still affects multiple aspects of public administration, from policy implementation to resource allocation and justice administration. This political interference reduces transparency and accountability, increasing public distrust in institutions and the state's ability to effectively manage the affairs within its purview. Additionally, politicization contributes to the creation of an inefficient bureaucracy, where appointments and promotions are usually not based on merit or competence but on political loyalties, which not only deteriorates the quality of public services but perpetuates a cycle of inefficiency and corruption. This results in a continuous degradation of institutional integrity, where short-term focus and lack of strategic vision limit the country's capacity to address its structural challenges.

For the case at hand, in a quick assessment of the situation, the protocols suggested in the manuals were not applicable. Often, before authorizing a rescue mission, it is necessary to complete a preliminary assessment that includes gathering information, coordinating between various agencies, and obtaining permits to operate in remote areas. Although these steps are designed to ensure the efficient use of resources and operational safety, it was evident that they would significantly delay the arrival of teams at the accident site.

Response speed is a critical factor, and search and rescue protocols, when applied without discernment and burdened with bureaucracy, can cause fatal delays, endangering the life of a pilot who, in extreme conditions, may not have the time necessary to survive while awaiting rescue.

Therefore, and without attempting to be redundant, to mitigate these risks, search and rescue protocols must be reviewed and adapted to the realities of mountain operations. This could include simplifying certain procedures, delegating more authority to local rescue teams, and integrating technology that enables a faster and more precise response. Ultimately, the priority must always be the pilot's life, ensuring that speed and efficiency are not compromised by bureaucracy.

In the situation described here, following our landing in Cholila, we received a communication informing us that the airspace in the search area for the lost pilot in the mountains would be closed. This decision, made by the competent authority, prompted our immediate objection. It is well known that, in a mountainous search operation, having more resources and specialized personnel considerably increases the chances of successfully locating a missing person.

Our intention was to request the immediate mobilization of the Cessna 172 from El Bolsón and to call an instructor pilot to command the Cessna 152 from Trevelin belonging to the company Patagonia Bush Pilot, both planes with experienced mountain pilots familiar with the area and accustomed to the complexities that this type of operation presents. Each of us would be accompanied by observers, also qualified, as the pilot primarily needs to control the aircraft, focusing on flight parameters that prevent them from fully observing the terrain.

Our disagreement with the airspace closure was met with a surprisingly dismissive response from the authority who issued it: "Instead of looking for one, we'll end up looking for two or three." This comment not only underestimated our capabilities but also unfairly questioned our professionalism. Are mountain pilots not capable of maintaining appropriate flight levels? Are we not able to coordinate our actions and communicate effectively? This reasoning implies that we are reckless, incompetent novices, which is not only untrue but also an insult to our dedication and training. Mountain pilots, especially in search and rescue situations, operate with a high sense of responsibility and a deep commitment to safety, and we have always willingly devoted our time and resources to acts of solidarity. It is precisely our training, experience, and ability to act under pressure that make us fit to face the challenges of this type of mission.

This reminded me of an earlier incident at the Aeroclub Bariloche when we received the news that Gustavo Salamida, an instructor at the institution, had had an accident during takeoff with a Lake Buccaneer, an amphibious aircraft, from El Totoral Lagoon near Villa La Angostura. We immediately organized a team of pilots and went to the accident site with an inflatable boat.

A team of divers was already in the area, trying to locate the plane and the pilot. The passengers onboard had managed to escape in time before the aircraft sank. The survivors recounted that Gustavo had given up his own life jacket to a passenger who could not swim.

When we arrived, we were flatly denied the chance to assist, with the explanation that we might interfere with the professional work already underway. However, after a day of fruitless search efforts by the divers, we were finally given permission to enter the lake. Our team had a rudimentary fish finder, originally designed for locating fish, a tool far from ideal but nonetheless useful for the situation we were facing. We analyzed the conditions of the area, taking into account the prevailing wind direction, the size of the lagoon, and the factors Gustavo would have considered when selecting the takeoff path given the available surface and the wind direction and speed.

We established a search pattern with a zigzag trajectory, covering the probable flight path based on aeronautical principles dictating the best exit options in such a confined scenario. The lakebed had a homogeneous topography; it was a flat basin without plants, rocks, or logs that might interfere with the sonar readings. Shortly after, we found some of the aircraft's documents floating, safely stored in sealed plastic covers. Shortly after, the fish finder screen displayed the unmistakable silhouette of the inverted plane on the lakebed.

We marked the position and notified the divers, who, upon reaching the wreckage, confirmed that the aircraft was empty. Several days passed before Gustavo's body was found near one of the shores, bringing an end to a search that could have been expedited had the input of pilots with technical knowledge of maneuvers and aeronautical procedures in emergency situations been valued.

This event highlights once again how qualified human resources are often underutilized, underestimating the technical skills of those who, like us in that situation, were in a position to contribute a specialized approach. Aviation experience not only includes knowledge of flight, but also factors such as local meteorology, aircraft behavior on different surfaces and environments, and critical decision-making. These aspects are inherent in pilot training, so their participation can significantly contribute to rescue tasks, with an adequate interpretation of the environment and the most probable aeronautical maneuvers. Preventing that collaboration and dismissing these capabilities helped to prolong the search, when from the outset, we could have assisted in delineating the most probable area where the aircraft was located.

There is a continuous sentiment expressed on social media, in groups that bring together general aviation pilots, and at aeronautical gatherings, that there is a noticeable disregard for the sector by various bodies within aviation administration. The feeling conveyed is that they would feel more comfortable with the absence of this segment. It's as if their presence were a constant nuisance, an unwanted interruption whenever a pilot tries to access a controlled airport, refuel, occupy a spot on the apron, or request an overnight stay.

However, it is only fair to acknowledge that in many airports we are pleasantly surprised by controllers or Flight Plan staff who are fully aware that they are providing a service to aviation. Far from displaying an authoritarian or dismissive attitude, they are very attentive and professional when it comes to providing assistance.

It is necessary to recognize that this category of general aviation not only constitutes the majority of the aviation sector in Argentina but has also been and continues to be, the fundamental foundation upon which aviation in the country was developed.

Aeroclubs have historically been the "seedbeds" where the pilots who now operate the largest and most sophisticated aircraft of commercial airlines were trained. These small planes have been the tools through which these professionals acquired their first flight hours, honed their skills, and built their aviation careers.

And regarding the topic at hand, these institutions, spread throughout the country, are always ready to contribute, able to immediately provide their well-suited aircraft, as they are low-speed planes, and at least two or three very experienced pilots familiar with the area due to their local roots.

In specialized media, it is increasingly noted with concern that there is a shortage of trained pilots in Argentina, which could affect the country's aviation industry if steps are not taken to improve training and attract more people to the profession.

Despite this context, there is a widespread underestimation of this group, fueled by inaccurate perceptions and biases about their abilities. There is a recurrent tendency to view these pilots as a "non-professional" segment, wrongly assuming that they lack the expertise, technical skill, and discipline necessary to fly safely and efficiently. This judgment, which oversimplifies and distorts reality, affects both the pilot's confidence and the recognition they receive from the broader aviation community.

This attitude is clearly manifested in a series of measures that, under the guise of ensuring safety, create an overly controlling environment. The regulations imposed on this group often seem unnecessarily restrictive, more aimed at limiting their activity than promoting their development and improving operational safety. This excess of regulations and their relentless application, far from fostering a safe environment, increases pressure on the pilot, creating situations where excessive oversight can become counterproductive.

Frequent admonitions, often perceived as unnecessary or disproportionate, only serve to heighten stress in the cockpit. In addition to facing the already demanding tasks of navigation, communication, and aircraft control, pilots often have to contend with a watchful attitude that, instead of providing support, creates an atmosphere of mistrust. The interaction with air traffic controllers, which should be a tool for assistance and safety, is affected by this climate of scrutiny, generating nervousness that can compromise judgment and decision-making in critical moments.

In some cases, this situation has escalated to the point of prompting public complaints in specialized forums where pilots share their frustrations and negative experiences. The complaints vary, but all point to the lack of respect and the dismissive treatment they receive from some authorities. These forums have served as an outlet, but also as a platform to raise awareness about the impacts such attitudes can have on operational safety. Instead of fostering an environment of collaboration and continuous improvement, the strict control and distrust erode the pilot's focus, a distraction that can be dangerous, especially during the most delicate phases of flight, such as takeoff, landing, or in adverse weather conditions.

This issue underscores the urgent need to review control and oversight policies, promoting a more balanced approach based on mutual trust. The training and experience of these pilots should be recognized and valued appropriately, as many have demonstrated skills and abilities that not only meet but exceed standards, bringing to aviation a different but equally valuable perspective.

The reality is that general aviation and small aircraft play an essential role not only in training pilots but also in maintaining a vibrant and accessible aeronautical culture throughout the country. Ignoring its importance or underestimating its value is not only unfair, but it also risks the sustainability and growth of the aviation sector in Argentina. It is imperative that aviation authorities recognize and adequately value this segment, fostering an environment where all aviation stakeholders, regardless of their size or reach, can coexist and thrive for the benefit of national aviation.

The Search

Finally, night quickly fell over Cholila, wrapping the landscape in a shroud of darkness that seemed to amplify the exhaustion accumulated from a grueling day. Every muscle ached, but the most difficult burden to bear was the weight of responsibility. Our next steps had to be precise and effective to help save our friend's life. Part of it rested in our hands, though his survival depended mostly on him — on his physical and mental resilience, his ability to endure such a tremendous ordeal.

We gathered in the cabin provided for us, a temporary shelter that offered some respite from the harsh elements outside. The warmth of coffee in our hands was comforting, a small luxury amid the uncertainty surrounding us. Yet we couldn't surrender to rest; our minds kept working, organizing, planning, thinking about the next step.

In a situation like this, the mountain, with its imposing majesty, where nature displays its full grandeur and splendor, ceases to be just a simple landscape or a physical obstacle; it becomes an opponent that won't easily yield ground. With every gust of wind, with every layer of snow falling, it seemed to come alive, as if rising to remind us of our fragility in the face of its power, joining forces with time, which now became another relentless enemy. In this struggle, we were all being tested — Queque most of all, demanding the best from each of us, not only in terms of technical skill or physical endurance but also in terms of mental and emotional strength. This situation revealed multiple fronts: against the fury of the elements, human limitations, and sometimes, against one's own instinct suggesting retreat.

I needed my agenda, which I had left in the plane, so I immediately got up to retrieve it. As I opened the door and stepped out from the warm shelter, the impact was immediate and brutal. The cold hit me like a punch, sharp and unforgiving, accompanied by icy rain that seemed to pierce down to the bone.

At that moment, the image of Queque, facing that same storm without any shelter, etched itself in my mind, and a sense of discouragement began to creep in. How could he withstand it? How could anyone, soaked to the bone, with equipment ill-suited to these conditions and surrounded by utter darkness, maintain not only physical strength but also hope? As I walked to the plane, each drop of rain was a reminder of the hostility of the environment, of the battle Queque was fighting alone somewhere in that vast, dark, desolate expanse.

And if down here, at 1,800 feet above sea level, it was raining, it was surely snowing at 5,000 feet, with a merciless and icy snow that not only drenched but drained energy, robbed warmth, leaving him vulnerable in a night where warmth was the line between life and death.

I knew of many who, in a similar situation, had considered surrendering, ceasing to fight, experiencing an almost comforting sensation in doing so. I hoped he would keep fighting, but it was a great test of internal strength. There are many cases of strong individuals who break under the combination of physical exhaustion, extreme cold, and the despair that seeps into the mind when everything seems lost.

I put myself in his place, trying to feel what he would be feeling. Queque, being an informed pilot, was surely aware of the severity of his situation. He knew that the next day's weather conditions would be very adverse, and an aerial rescue was, at best, uncertain. How, then, could he keep his spirits up, knowing that every passing minute moved him further away from the hope of a rescue? How could he resist the temptation to give in, to surrender to fatigue, to the cold, to loneliness? The darkness surrounding him was not just of the night, but of uncertainty, of not knowing if he would ever see the light of a new day.

I stopped in the rain, feeling the cold seep into my soul, as if nature itself wanted to challenge my will, pushing me toward despair. Every drop that fell seemed to carry a fragment of will, eroding it slowly. Yet, in that moment of apparent weakness, though overwhelmed by helplessness, something stronger emerged: a renewed determination. We could not, we must not, fail. Finding Queque transcended us; his life, his existence was intertwined with so many others — his family, his community in Trevelin, those of us who shared a passion for flying, and our general aviation segment with small aircraft. Right now, Queque was not just a friend lost in the mountains; he was a symbol of what it means to belong to a brotherhood forged in the sky and adversity. We had to transmit energy to him, strength that we needed to channel toward him even from afar. We also recognized the need to synchronize our minds, not only to hold on a little longer but to make the most accurate decisions.

We needed to make him feel he wasn't alone; though the storm enveloped him in an icy embrace, he had to feel that we were here, resisting with him, fighting the same enemy in our own way. Each of us, from our different positions and roles, pushing with all our strength, driven by a single motivation: not to let the mountain take the life of one of our own. Just as he couldn't give in to despair, neither could we relent in our efforts. The strength of determination, of camaraderie, of love for life, had to rise above adversity, and in that moment, I felt we would bring him back.

I returned to the cabin and went over the contacts. There, in WhatsApp groups and emails, were many names. Behind each one lay an extensive network of camaraderie, some shared stories, skills, expertise, and connections. We made a selection and began calling.

Once we brought our friends up to speed, a domino effect was set in motion. Immediately, names, resources, and funds were made available from unimaginable places, including communications from Alaska. It was challenging at first, but we managed to coordinate and assign roles. Our primary, very clear objective was to secure a helicopter, a suitable aircraft, and a crew with mountain knowledge.

Before long, we had three options, but we chose the one suggested by Juan Martín Escobar and Reinaldo Vandonselar, who contacted a crew from a private company in San Martín de los Andes.

They had a Bell 407, ideal for the mission, a robust aircraft with great maneuverability and a large four-blade rotor. And most importantly, the pilots were seasoned in this type of terrain. In fact, their work involved heli-ski excursions, tourism, and mountain rescues. They also knew the area, having recently been to Cholila with skiers, and their experience in mountain flying made them our first and best option.

The response was immediate. No doubts, no unnecessary questions. The situation was clear: a person, colleague, and friend needed a rescue, and it had to be done as quickly as possible.

When I spoke with Tomy Bosio, he inspired a lot of confidence, not only due to his willingness but also because I realized, through his questions and assessment of the actions to follow, that he was a true professional. His firmness didn't come from arrogance but from experience, from having been in similar situations.

Beyond planning the flight details, he showed an ability to consider the collateral aspects involved in the entire rescue mission.

After speaking with him and coordinating for the next day, I felt our chances of success, though still uncertain, had increased considerably.

In this case, we knew precisely where the accident had occurred, knew the pilot was in reasonably good physical condition, were aware of the route he was taking down, and the likely spots where he would camp. We needed to concentrate on rescuing a person in the mountains, not on searching for the plane.

The forecast indicated that the next day would bring marginal weather conditions, with persistent rain and low clouds likely to complicate any aerial operation. However, we had agreed that the pilot would take off at first light from San Martín de los Andes, coordinating with us beforehand to obtain a precise, real-time weather update.

Meanwhile, the rescue and logistics team, comprising Steven Williams and José Beccar, trained mountaineers, were in Villa La Angostura attending a mountain operations course. Without hesitation, they interrupted their training and packed all necessary equipment into a truck to drive to Cholila that very night. They understood time was a critical factor, so they started the journey immediately, arriving at our meeting point by two in the morning. This early arrival was crucial, as it gave us the necessary hours to better plan the rescue operation for the following day.

Simultaneously, and anticipating that weather conditions could prevent the helicopter from flying, a ground patrol was organized for the early morning. We arranged for a boat to cross Lake Cholila and depart from its western end, which would allow more direct access to the search area. However, Walter Marchand, a seasoned tracker with extensive knowledge of the terrain, suggested it would be safer and more efficient to use his 4x4 truck. Despite the precarious condition of the road skirting the lake, his experience indicated they could advance a few additional kilometers past the lake's tip, which would not only shorten the search distance but also offer greater protection if we found the missing person, given the extreme cold in the area.

This decision held great tactical importance, as in such a hostile environment, every kilometer gained and every accurate measure significantly increased the chances of a successful rescue mission.

Dawn was slow to arrive. In the depths of winter, nights are very long at these latitudes. But conditions, though not ideal for the search, would allow the helicopter pilot to make the journey. We connected by phone, gave him our report, and suggested a route across the steppe, skirting Bariloche, over Ñorquinco and El Maitén, approaching from the east through one of the large valleys in Cholila without needing to cross mountainous elevations. The west and north were completely blocked by weather.

Shortly, the helicopter was in flight, and after just under two hours, the distinctive sound of its rotors approaching resonated like a melody of hope in our ears. The pilots, Tomy Bosio and Hernán Fabbio, made a flawless landing in a specially prepared area, carefully avoiding interference with the landing strip, which had to be kept clear for the operation of the Cessna 180 or other aircraft that might join the search mission. Every detail counted, and every move was calculated and evaluated to maximize our options.

The Patagonia Bush Pilots team, Queque's close friends and support crew, had already gathered at the site, forming a cohesive unit driven by a single objective: to find their companion. The worry and determination were evident in their faces, and we all waited anxiously for the sky to clear enough to allow an effective search operation.

The helicopter, having consumed a significant amount of

fuel during its journey from its base, needed to refuel to conduct an extended search. Esquel was the nearest place for refueling, requiring a temporary pause in our search activities. Initially, the plan was for the helicopter to head directly to the airfield to refuel, and once resupplied, return to begin the full search operations.

However, given the proximity of the area where we suspected Queque might be, we insisted on a different strategy. We proposed that instead of flying directly to Esquel, the helicopter conduct an initial flyover of the search area, deviating slightly en route to refuel. Although the chances of locating him on this first attempt were slim, we knew that the mere fact of a helicopter passing over the area would send a powerful message: "A helicopter is in the area and is looking for you."

This flyover would have significant psychological impact. It would not only lift Queque's spirits, letting him know that rescue efforts were underway, but also give him the opportunity to position himself in a more visible and accessible location for the aircraft. He could lay out materials to facilitate his location, better manage his resources, and be reassured that rescue was imminent. Although simple in appearance, this maneuver carried deep meaning.

Another option, if he wasn't spotted from the helicopter on that initial flight and we noticed he had moved into the woods, was for the rescuers to ski down his tracks with dry clothing, provisions, and a radio to help him reach a place where the helicopter could land. This plan was put on standby for possible use in the afternoon if the search intensified with better weather.

Our uncertainty about Queque's condition was immense, and our anxiety grew. Every few minutes, I would step outside to check the sky. The plane was ready, and I would take off as soon as conditions allowed. However, I watched with concern as the wind intensified at higher altitudes; clouds over the mountain were moving fast, and the area we needed to fly over was turbulent, with many downdrafts and very unstable air currents, making it difficult to reach Cerro Plataforma.

Although we were confident he had headed toward Cholila, there was a possibility he might have taken the route to Puelo, which had a marked trail and was the more frequented path, though farther away. My plan was to fly over the area to locate any tracks, which would inform us of his intended path and determine which route he had taken down the mountain to locate him. Additionally, knowing that the helicopter could only make one pass, I would try to locate him and provide coordinates for the other aircraft to proceed efficiently.

As soon as we could take off, I went up first to try to locate him and guide the helicopter. Bernardo Braig accompanied me as the observer, while Pablo, my son, would be in the helicopter to help them pinpoint the likely location where Queque was sheltered or walking.

We took off and had to fly quite high due to turbulence and downdrafts, and also to leave space below for the helicopter. We entered over the canyon separating Cerro Plataforma from Tres Picos and saw that the snowfall had erased all tracks. Queque was directly below us, but we couldn't see him. We crossed through the blowing snow to the Turbio Valley and returned over the mountain. We radioed the helicopter, now airborne, to report that visibility conditions were good and that we hadn't seen any tracks.

The helicopter moved forward at low altitude and slow speed, examining every meter of the surface. The two pilots, experienced in extreme rescue operations, kept their eyes fixed on the terrain, scanning for any sign of the orange plastic that would indicate Queque's position. Pablo, seated behind them, also observed from his position with immense focus, fully aware that this was the moment of truth, his heart in his throat, torn between hope and fear.

As they approached the designated area, while Tomy guided the helicopter, Hernán, the other pilot, as if reading his mind, turned to him with a calm but weighty voice carrying the gravity of someone experienced in such situations. He asked with the calm of one who had seen all sides of tragedy, "Are you prepared for what we might find? There's a chance your friend may not have survived, and we may have to bring him back outside on the rack, frozen."

These words hit Pablo like a blast of icy wind. It was a truth that everyone on the team had considered in some corner of their minds, yet few dared to voice. However, each time that thought surfaced, they rejected it with firm conviction and confidence in Queque's ability to survive. They relied on his resilience, his mental strength, his intimate knowledge of the mountains and snow. Queque wasn't a novice; he was a snowboard instructor, and the snow was a familiar element to him.

Nonetheless, reality was relentless. They knew what he was going through—desperate conditions, inadequate equipment to withstand the mountain's harsh elements. The cold was severe, and the snow, beyond its chill, made each step exhausting and physically demanding. Despite their faith in his endurance, the possibility of finding him in critical condition, or worse, couldn't be ignored. The harshness of the situation became increasingly palpable as the helicopter approached the accident site.

For years, we had followed the series "Flying Wild Alaska" with fascination—a visual account of life in that remote, inhospitable land, where Jim Tweto and his family had built an air service that became an essential component for multiple communities. With a fleet of small planes, Tweto and his team connected isolated northern villages, transporting fishermen, hunters, and delivering vital supplies to places where survival would otherwise be challenging.

The series showcased Alaska's extreme, wild beauty and

highlighted the inherent risks of flying in one of the world's most untamed environments. Each flight was a mission in itself, facing not only distances and the lack of infrastructure but also unpredictable weather, hostile geography, and the constant need for critical, high-stakes decision-making under pressure.

Yet beyond the adventure, what stood out in Jim Tweto was his deep concern for the safety of his pilots and crew. In each rescue, in every challenging flight, his primary fear wasn't merely the possibility of a forced landing or an accident; it was what could happen afterward. To Tweto, the real danger materialized if a pilot or crew was forced to spend the night exposed to Alaska's unforgiving climate.

Tweto understood that nature is unyielding and that one night without shelter in the middle of nowhere could be deadly. Sub-zero temperatures, snow, and freezing winds represented an extreme risk, in his view surpassing even the immediate consequences of an accident. He knew that prolonged exposure to those elements could end in a tragedy far worse than the forced landing that may have triggered the emergency in the first place.

Sadly, Jim Tweto died in an accident in his famous Cessna 180, N91361, on June 26, 2023, near Shaktoolik, a small community on Alaska's west coast.

Drawing parallels between Jim Tweto's story and his company in Alaska with the operations of Patagonia Bush Pilots is inevitable, revealing a connection between two regions so distant but so similar in their essence. Both stories unfold in landscapes governed by nature. The difference lies in the freedom to fly in the northern country, which allows it to flourish, whereas excessive restrictions in the southern country prevent using these tools for connection, survival, and rescue in remote settings.

Pablo and Queque had visited Alaska a month before this incident, interacting with other bush pilots, learning from their experiences, their flying techniques, aircraft modifications, and adaptations with the intent of replicating them in Patagonia.

Patagonia presents a similar scene to Alaska—a vast and isolated territory where mountains, valleys, and lakes form a natural ensemble that pilots must navigate amidst unpredictable weather, strong winds, and irregular topography. Distances are great, towns are far apart, and there are few roads. For this reason, bush flying in the region could play an essential role in community service, transporting vital supplies, connecting people in these remote corners, and, in critical situations, performing rescues in heavy snowfalls, floods, or assisting the sick or disabled.

If my Cessna had been equipped with skis—something not permitted under Argentine aeronautical regulations—I would have landed right there, picked up the pilot, and taken him to a place where he could recover immediately.

The helicopter moved forward slowly for better observation. A person standing in dark clothing would be invisible among the leafless trees. Their hope centered on spotting the orange plastic. Suddenly, a splotch of that color against the pristine white landscape caught their attention, but it turned out to be a drum near one of the last outposts before entering the mountains. It appeared out of nowhere, sparking a brief wave of hope among the crew. They were gripped by the illusion that they had found Queque, but reality soon set in. It was a false alarm. Still, the situation was not entirely in vain: they confirmed that the orange color was highly visible against the snow in that light.

The aircraft continued its course, slicing through the cold air as it flew over a lenga forest, its bare branches stripped of leaves by winter, where every shadow, every nook beneath the trees seemed to hide him like a buried mirage. And then, the miracle they had longed for finally happened. In a perfect clearing, as if nature had aligned with them for a moment and opened up a space to receive them, they saw him. There, in the snow, was Queque, arms raised, holding up an orange plastic sheet—the signal of life they had been hoping for.

For everyone, time seemed to stand still. The image of Queque was small but incredibly meaningful in the vast landscape, filling everyone with emotion. He was alive. Against all odds, he had survived. Tomy, the pilot, immediately understood the significance of the moment and switched on the landing lights, a silent gesture that conveyed: "We see you, you're safe now." Then, he initiated the landing maneuver, carefully bringing down the helicopter to carry out the rescue that had been planned with such care and hope.

To ensure a safe landing, the helicopter had to position itself against the wind, which required passing over Queque's location, stretching those last seconds before final contact. As he listened to the rotor blades slicing through the air and felt the aircraft descending slowly, Queque's emotions were a mix of hope and anxious anticipation. Suddenly, everything started to unfold like a slow-motion scene in a movie—as if he were not the main character but a spectator with a privileged view of the unfolding plot. It wasn't just a visual effect; the sounds also seemed to slow—the rhythmic thump of the blades, the unmistakable "Whop, Whop" of the rotors' air displacement—each seemed to stretch out in time.

The moment the skids touched the snow felt like a chapter closing. Just a few meters now separated him from the helicopter, and at that precise moment, his internal battle—the one he had fought against the cold, solitude, and fear—came to an end.

The adrenaline that had kept him going during those endless hours, like an invisible armor holding him up, suddenly abandoned him. He felt his energy drain from his body, like a balloon slowly deflating until it was completely empty. The strength that had sustained and propelled him up to that moment vanished abruptly, and with the certainty that he was now safe, his legs refused to take another step.

As Hernán kept the helicopter engine running, Tomy jumped out with a mix of urgency and joy, running toward Queque. The emotion of the moment was so overwhelming that he couldn't resist the urge to capture it with a selfie, immortalizing the instant when the fight for survival turned into a moment of relief. Despite his extreme exhaustion, the rescued pilot managed a weak but genuinely heartfelt smile.

Carefully, they helped him into the helicopter. To his immense relief, he saw that Pablo was seated inside and came over to embrace him, showing his own sense of relief. Although Queque was visibly exhausted, his overall condition was surprisingly good for someone who had survived such harsh conditions. His hands wouldn't stop trembling, not so much from the cold he had endured but from the overwhelming mix of emotions: the relief of being alive, the mental exhaustion of maintaining hope, and the simple gratitude of being back.

As the helicopter took off again, leaving behind the landscape that had been almost his prison during those endless hours, he took a moment to close his eyes and let the sound of the rotor blades—a kind of marvelous rhythm—envelop him in a sense of safety.

They decided to take him to the cabin set up for them in Cholila, a cozy refuge offering a welcome respite after the ordeal he had endured. The aim was to provide him with a space where he could have something warm and regain his strength before continuing his journey to Trevelin, where his family was waiting. In Esquel, an emergency team had prepared an area near the hospital to receive

El Bell 407 de IBEX

the helicopter, ready in case Queque needed urgent treatment for hypothermia.

Upon arriving at the cabin, the logs burning in the hearth crackled loudly, as if celebrating Queque's return to a safe and warm environment. The sound of the fire created a comforting atmosphere, while the warmth of the home, combined with dry clothes and a hot soup, began to restore the vitality he had lost during his ordeal. Little by little, the bluish tint of his legs and arms, evidence of the intense cold he had endured, began to fade. However, the aftereffects of his exposure to such low temperatures lingered for several more days, a persistent reminder of the adversity he had faced.

Once his condition stabilized, and although he still felt the aches in his body and the emotional weight of his experience, he was transported to Trevelin.

As he neared the meeting point with his family, the scene was a whirlwind of emotions. From the helicopter's window, Queque could spot in the distance the figures he had longed for so deeply—their image had sustained him. There they were, his wife and daughter, standing still but with their eyes fixed on the sky, desperately searching for the machine that would bring back the husband and father they had feared losing.

When the helicopter touched down, and as they waited for the rotor blades to stop spinning, Queque, still trembling from the cold and adrenaline, had the door opened for him. With unsteady steps, he approached his family and melted into an embrace that encapsulated everything they had been through. It was a hug that blended anguish, relief, and the need to erase the time of uncertainty and emotional pain while he was lost and anchor themselves in this new reality of being together again.

Finally, in a trembling voice, he managed to articulate the

Hernán Fabbio
Tommy Bosio

words, "I'm here… I'm safe." A simple yet profound phrase in the context of what had happened, resonating like a balm and carrying away the weight of all he had suffered.

His friends and the helicopter pilots, the silent heroes of that day, watched from a distance with a mix of satisfaction at a job well done and exhaustion from the hours of effort. Knowing that this family reunion would not have been possible without their participation, they felt, from their second-row vantage point, that this moment also belonged to them.

That night, as the starry sky spread over Trevelin and the winter cold returned—this time finding him in the warmth of his home—Queque reflected on the thin line separating life from death. That accident had been a brutal test, a moment when nature had shown him its most unforgiving face. But he had triumphed, through his tenacity, the bond with his family that gave him resilience, and the unyielding efforts of his friends who refused to stop until they brought him back.

Deep within himself, he knew his life would never be the same again. He had survived not only to tell his story but to live it fully, with renewed gratitude and love. In that starlit silence, he felt the mountain had not taken anything from him but had instead returned to him the true value of every moment.

Thus, a story of survival was sealed, forever etched into the memory of everyone involved.

CHAPTER 4
TECHNICAL ASPECTS

In this chapter, a more exhaustive analysis alternates between detailed descriptions and summaries of various topics addressed throughout the account of the epic journey in the mountains. This approach allows for an in-depth exploration of the key technical aspects that must be considered when planning and executing flights with small aircraft in mountainous environments.

This includes aircraft preparation, emphasizing the importance of conducting thorough preflight inspections to ensure structural integrity and mechanical performance under extreme conditions. Additionally, it addresses the procedures for load and fuel adjustments to optimize balance and range, critical aspects when routes require precision maneuvers and minimal margins for error.

The text delves into navigation through peaks and valleys, highlighting the need to interpret updrafts and downdrafts, as well as anticipating the influence of orographic winds and turbulence generated by mountainous formations. Specific maneuvers are detailed, such as steep turns to change direction in confined spaces, chandelles to gain altitude on steep slopes, and controlled descents to navigate narrow passes.

Engine operation is a focal point, particularly in managing the fuel-air mixture, monitoring engine temperature, and keeping track of critical indicators to ensure reliable performance at high altitudes. Technologies that facilitate these operations are also discussed, such as GPS with topographic maps, weather alert systems, and advanced instruments that provide greater precision in decision-making.

Lastly, considerations are included for other factors that, although often taken for granted, are essential for ensuring the safety and efficiency of mountain flying. These include planning alternative routes, analyzing potential emergency landing sites, and the importance of specialized training to prepare pilots for unforeseen challenges in a hostile environment.

Thus, this chapter aims not only to provide a technical guide but also to highlight the connection between preparation, knowledge, and the pilot's ability to overcome the challenges of mountain flying.

FLIGHT PLANNING

To organize a flight over the mountains in a single-engine aircraft, a series of considerations must be addressed, including studying the complexity of the terrain, variable weather conditions, and the specific challenges of mountain flying. A detailed plan spans from terrain analysis to emergency procedures and real-time monitoring, integrating knowledge of aerial navigation, meteorology, and survival skills.

1. Terrain and Route Analysis

. Review of Aeronautical Charts and Maps
Before flying over the Patagonian Andes, analyzing detailed aeronautical charts and topographic maps is essential. These resources provide precise understanding of elevations, peaks, depressions, and valleys, as well as geographical features that serve as landmarks. The Patagonian Andes feature unique elements such as glaciers, glacial lakes, and wide riverbeds, which can aid in orientation and position confirmation along the flight route.

. Visual Landmarks and Alternate Routes

In rugged terrain, visual landmarks are crucial. While flying over the Andes, prominent geographic features (e.g., Mount Fitz Roy or Cerro Torre) serve as visual checkpoints. Additionally, it is advisable to anticipate alternate routes in case unfavorable weather or other contingencies necessitate a course change. Identifying nearby airstrips or, at a minimum, flat safe areas for emergency landings is critical. In the Andes, where weather changes rapidly and visibility may be limited, having well-defined escape routes is essential.

. Safe Passages

The Patagonian Andes have well-known passes used

by experienced pilots that offer some protection against strong wind currents and lower elevations. Planning should prioritize these natural passes to cross the range without requiring excessive altitude and minimizing exposure to intense turbulence.

2. Weather Conditions Analysis

. Mountain Weather Forecast

The Andean region of Patagonia is renowned for its variable and often adverse weather conditions. Obtaining a specific mountain forecast, including wind direction and speed at each altitude level, atmospheric temperatures, and the likelihood of adverse conditions such as snowfall or thunderstorms, is essential. The forecast should be analyzed in advance and, if possible, just before takeoff to assess last-minute changes.

.Orographic Wind Considerations

Mountains generate strong updrafts and downdrafts, known as mountain waves. In the Patagonian Andes, these waves can intensify due to the orientation of mountain chains and cold air masses from the Pacific. Downdrafts can push the aircraft toward the ground with force, requiring careful planning to maintain sufficient altitude and room for evasive maneuvers if necessary.

.Climate Variability and Visibility

Extreme weather variability can occur within minutes in this region. High cloud cover is common, and in winter, icing in clouds can present additional hazards. Poor visibility caused by fog, mountain mist, or heavy precipitation can prevent the pilot from maintaining visual contact with the terrain, increasing collision risks. It is crucial to have a clear understanding of expected weather throughout the flight and contingency plans.

3. Aircraft Performance Analysis

. Density Altitude

Density altitude directly affects engine performance and wing lift. At higher density altitudes, thinner air reduces both engine power and aerodynamic efficiency. This is critical for low-power single-engine aircraft. Calculating density altitude at different points along the route, especially near high passes or mountain ridges, is vital to avoid performance surprises.

.Climb Performance Calculation

Determining whether the aircraft can ascend to safe altitudes to clear mountainous terrain is fundamental. In the Andes, where some peaks exceed 3,000 meters, climb performance must be calculated under various load and weather conditions. Having the ability to execute steep turns and maintain power on steep inclines ensures that a ridge can be cleared or a pass navigated when necessary.

.Fuel Consumption Planning

Fuel consumption may increase significantly during mountain flights due to maneuvers and higher fuel burn during climbs. Additionally, high-altitude flight can affect fuel efficiency based on density altitude and wind conditions. Carrying an additional fuel margin, typically 15–20% more than estimated, is crucial for these flights.

4. Load Preparation

.Weight Limitation

The altitude and need for climbing maneuvers or steep turns demand that the aircraft be in optimal weight conditions. Minimizing the load allows the aircraft to respond better to controls and maintain climbing capability.

. Survival Equipment

The aircraft should carry appropriate survival equipment for a potential prolonged stay in the mountains, including warm clothing, water, non-perishable food, a medical kit, a portable radio, and a flashlight. These items can make a critical difference in case of an emergency landing. A list adapted to the Patagonian region is described later in this book.

. Weight Distribution and Balance

Even load distribution and securing are vital, as shifting weight in tight spaces or turbulent conditions could upset the aircraft's balance. Proper weight distribution, maintaining the center of gravity, enhances maneuverability and responsiveness to environmental conditions.

5. Emergency Procedures

Practicing specific emergency procedures, such as steep turns, chandelles, or low-speed flying in safe zones, is beneficial. During flight planning, identify flat areas or valleys on the map where an emergency landing can be executed. Ideally, snowfields, flat terrains such as meadows, beaches, or creek edges are preferred.

6. Establish Communication Networks and Emergency Protocols

Mountain communication may be limited due to geographical interference. Carrying an emergency radio and devices such as locator beacons can facilitate rescue in case of an incident. Having a clear communication protocol with family or friends monitoring the flight and knowledge of mountain rescue frequencies is essential.

7. Flight Itinerary Reporting

Reporting the flight itinerary to the control tower or a trusted contact is good practice. This itinerary should include the route, checkpoints, expected duration, and potential diversion points. In case of lost communication or signal, the rescue team can know where to search.

8. GPS System and Checkpoint Verification

Carrying an updated GPS system with detailed mountain maps allows real-time position monitoring, altitude verification, and staying on course, especially in low-visibility conditions. Pre-marked visual checkpoints on the chart help confirm the aircraft's position and adjust the course if necessary.

9. Continuous In-Flight Checks

During the flight, continuous checks of the environment and the aircraft are crucial. These include verifying altitude, wind direction and speed, and weather conditions. Timely evaluation of any changes allows immediate adjustments to avoid entering dangerous conditions.

10. Post-Flight Evaluation and Logging

To accumulate experience, maintaining a log of encountered conditions, areas of turbulence, identification of updrafts and downdrafts, aircraft behavior, fuel consumption, time spent in specific circuits, and noteworthy situations is highly useful. This log serves to refine strategies for future flights, share insights with other pilots, and enhance mountain flight safety.

PRE-FLIGHT INSPECTION

The pre-flight inspection of an aircraft is a practice that contributes to the safety of the pilot, passengers, and the aircraft itself. This review, often referred to as a "preflight inspection" or "preflight check," consists of a systematic series of steps to evaluate the aircraft's condition before each flight, including the state of control surfaces, the engine, fuel systems, and the general structure of the aircraft, as well as the condition of instruments, electrical systems, and mechanical systems. Many issues can be detected during this inspection, potentially avoiding in-flight emergencies.

However, the inspection is not limited to mechanical aspects. It also involves checking the load, fuel levels, lubricants, mandatory onboard documents, and emergency equipment, ensuring the aircraft is ready for flight and providing the pilot with greater confidence to undertake it.

By incorporating this inspection practice as mandatory, rigorous, and systematic before flying, pilots minimize the risks associated with aviation.

Below is a standard procedure organized as a checklist. Some aspects not typically included in the manufacturer's manual must also be considered, such as tire pressure, cleaning insect debris or bird droppings from the windshield and other parts of the aircraft, nicks on the propeller, oil, fuel, or hydraulic fluid leaks—many of which can be observed from a distance—such as the alignment of ailerons or the aircraft's posture on a level surface.

Moreover, reading a checklist alone is insufficient, and some tools may be needed, such as a fuel tester cup to drain fuel, unscrewing inspection covers, a flashlight to observe the engine under the cowling, or cleaning the oil dipstick with a cloth or paper to measure accurately. Cleaning supplies for the windshield and a tire pressure gauge may also be required.

It is also necessary, if the aircraft was not hangared, to check for ice on the wings caused by humidity and overnight frost. While de-icing equipment and fluids may be available, the most practical method is often cleaning with warm water and drying afterward.

Beyond the exterior inspection, it is essential to perform a pre-start check and configuration inside the cockpit. This includes verifying instruments, ensuring fuel indicators match the visual inspection, setting the altimeter and compass, mounting the GPS or tablet if not fixed to the panel, and having headphones, a cell phone, maps, and notepads within reach. Additionally, check that the cargo is securely fastened in case of turbulence or sudden deceleration.

Detailed Pre-Flight Inspection Checklist

Cabin Inspection

- Verify that doors open and close easily, as difficulty may indicate misalignment or structural damage.
- Ensure the windshield is in good condition, clean, and free of cracks.
- Confirm that seats and seatbelts are in proper working condition, secure, and lock correctly in place.
- Check that ignition switches, magnetos, and battery are in the OFF position.
- Mixture control set to cut off.
- Propeller control: fully forward.

- Throttle control: idle.
- Altimeter set to field level.
- Verify that the fuel selector moves freely in all positions and return it to the appropriate tank.
- ELT must be in the armed position.
- Clean the windshield and windows as necessary.
- Verify the required documents and their validity.
- Lower flaps for exterior inspection.
- Confirm that GPS databases are up to date.
- Remove control locks.
- Engage the parking brake, if not already engaged.
- Ensure there are no loose items, and that the cargo is secured and evenly distributed.
- Check for the presence of a fire extinguisher, ensure it is adequately charged, inspected within the last year, and securely fastened.

Empennage

- Ensure it is secure. Check screws and hinges.
- Inspect surfaces for wrinkles or structural anomalies. Look for loose or missing rivets or fasteners.
- Verify the free movement of the elevator and rudder.
- Check tail lights and antennas.
- Inspect securing bolts.
- Check the tail skid, leaf spring, securing nuts, and tire condition (for conventional gear aircraft).

Right Wing

- Inspect the aileron for free movement in opposite directions; observe corresponding movement in the control yoke.
- Inspect flaps. Verify free movement and secure hinges and controls. Look for loose or missing screws, rivets, or fasteners.
- Inspect wing tips and lights for dents or cracks.
- Check the leading edge for dents or cracks.
- Visually check the fuel level, secure and lock fuel caps. The fuel quantity should match the expected amount based on the last flight/refueling. Fuel gauges should match visual inspection of the tanks.
- Look for fuel stains on the wing, along rivet lines (depending on the type of tank), and in areas where tanks are mounted, as these may indicate leaks.
- Use a fuel tester cup to check for water or debris in the fuel.

Main Landing Gear

- Remove tie-downs or chocks.
- Verify tire inflation, check for wear or bulges, ensure no lateral movement, and confirm the adjustment nut has a safety cotter pin.
- Inspect brakes, lines, calipers, and check for hydraulic fluid leaks.

Nose

- Open the cowling and inspect the engine for secure

spark plugs, wires, clamps, fuel injectors, and hoses. Check the fuel sump for leaks.

- Verify that drive belts have the correct tension and show no signs of wear.
- Ensure no foreign objects (such as bird or wasp nests) are inside, especially if the aircraft has been parked outdoors without cowling covers installed.
- Drain a small sample from the fuel filter into a transparent container to check for water or debris.
- Check engine oil levels, and if frequently flying the same aircraft, monitor for sudden increases in consumption or leaks.
- Secure the cowling cover with all screws in place. Clean the air filter if necessary.
- Inspect the propeller and spinner for damage. Move the propeller cautiously as if magnetos are live to avoid accidental ignition.
- Look for nicks or cracks and ensure each blade is securely fastened.
- Check for oil leaks in the propeller hub.
- Verify that the engine air intake is unobstructed.
- Inspect the nose wheel, tire, and proper inflation of the shock strut (for tricycle gear aircraft).

Left Wing

- Same as the right wing.
- Inspect the Pitot tube, remove the cover, and ensure it is unobstructed.

- Ensure the stall warning vane moves freely, is unobstructed, and the microswitch contact is audible.

Left Main Landing Gear

- Same as the right main gear.

Final Inspection

- Perform a final walkaround to ensure nothing has been left open, unsecured, or omitted from the pre-flight inspection.

This checklist is typically organized into different sections, including before engine start, before takeoff, sometimes during cruise, before landing, and after the aircraft is parked and shut down.

C180 CHECKLIST (1955)

1. BEFORE BOARDING THE AIRCRAFT
   Walk around and visually inspect the aircraft's general condition.
   Remove frost, mud, bird droppings, and insects.
   Remove Pitot cover and other protections.
   Remove tie-downs and tow bar.
   Drain fuel and check for water or debris.
   Check oil level and secure the dipstick.
   Visually verify fuel quantity and ensure caps are securely closed.
   Remove external and internal control locks.
   Ailerons: Inspect hinges and verify freedom of movement.
   Lower and inspect flaps.
   Check stall warning system.
   Tires: Check pressure and ensure safety pins are in place.

2. BEFORE STARTING THE ENGINE
   Complete preflight inspection.
   Seat belts: Buckled.
   Seats: Locked.
   Fuel selector: Both.
   Avionics power: Off.
   Circuit breakers: Checked.
   Cowl flaps: Open.
   ENGINE START
   Mixture: Full rich.
   Propeller pitch: High RPM.

Master switch: On.
Carburetor heat: Cold unless icing conditions exist.
Throttle: Open 1/2 inch.
Primer: 1 to 3 strokes.
Brakes: Set.
Magnetos: Both.
Starter switch: Engage.
Throttle: Reduce to 800–1000 RPM.
Oil pressure: Check.
Strobe lights: On.
Engine monitor: On.
Avionics master: On.
Navigation lights: Check.
Compass/DG: Verify.
ATIS: Record.
During taxi: Verify brakes, AI, and T&B.
Mixture: Lean for taxi.
If the engine is flooded, start with the throttle open and reduce after start.

3. BEFORE TAKEOFF
Doors: Secured.
Controls: Free and checked.
Instruments: Set and verified.
Altimeter: Set.
Verify compass and DG against runway heading.
Fuel selector: Both.
Fuel quantity: Check.
Mixture: Rich (or lean for altitude).
Trim: As required.
Cowl flaps: Open.
Engine Run-Up

Propeller: 1700 RPM.
Magnetos: Max drop of 100 RPM.
Carburetor heat: Check.
Propeller pitch: Check.
Suction pump: Check.
Ammeter: Check.
Radios: Set frequency.
Transponder: Set.
Strobe lights: On.
Flaps: 20°.

4. NORMAL TAKEOFF
   Pitot heat: Set.
   Apply full power.
   Propeller: Maximum RPM (fine pitch).
   Mixture: Rich.
   Liftoff: 70 mph.
   Clear obstacles: Maintain 85 mph with maximum power.
   Adjust power and RPM.

5. CLIMB
   Airspeed: 100 mph.
   Manifold pressure: 24".
   RPM: 2350.
   Cowl flaps: Open.
   Mixture: Rich.
   Retract flaps.

6. CRUISE
   Cowl flaps: Closed.
   Select power as required.
   Max manifold pressure: 23".
   RPM: 2400.
   Stabilize and adjust trim.
   Lean mixture per density altitude.
   Check instruments within green arc.

7. BEFORE LANDING
   Cowl flaps: Closed.
   Seat belts: Secured.
   Fuel selector: Both.
   Mixture: Rich.
   Propeller pitch: High RPM.
   Carburetor heat: On.
   Flaps: 10°–40°.
   Speeds:
   Approach: 90 mph.
   Final: 70 mph.
   Short field: 65 mph.

8. LANDING
   Normal landing: Three-point with full flaps.
   Apply brakes as needed to maintain control.
   Crosswind landing: Two-point on main wheels.
   If runway length permits, retract flaps.
   AFTER LANDING
   Flaps: Up.
   Cowl flaps: Open.
   Mixture: Lean for taxi.

9. ENGINE SHUTDOWN
   Avionics master: Off.
   Electrical switches: Off.
   Mixture: Idle cut-off.
   Magnetos: Off.
   Master switch: Off.
   Complete flight logs.

LOP FLIGHT TECHNIQUE

Aviation maintenance experts and piston engine specialists often criticize the old manuals that accompanied the purchase of aircraft for being overly simplified and brief. Mike Busch, one of the most renowned aviation mechanics, compares them to a cookbook. Busch dedicates most of his time to teaching the correct use of the mixture in piston engines, focusing on engine efficiency and longevity. As one of the most influential figures in the general aviation field, he is respected for his deep knowledge of aircraft maintenance and his advocacy for safer, more efficient, and economical operational practices. He has built a reputation as one of the most trusted experts on the proper use and care of aviation engines, particularly piston engines.

One of Busch's most significant contributions to the aviation world is his emphasis on educating aircraft owners. He firmly believes that pilots and aircraft owners must thoroughly understand the technical aspects of their airplanes, which includes detailed knowledge of both preventive and corrective maintenance. For him, this understanding not only enhances safety but can also lead to significant cost savings by enabling owners to make more informed decisions about maintenance and repairs.

Busch has authored books and numerous technical articles on aircraft maintenance, many of which have been published in renowned aviation magazines such as AOPA Pilot and AVweb. His ability to demystify complex technical concepts and make them accessible to a broader audience is one of the reasons for his popularity within the aviation community. Through his writings, Busch has addressed a wide range of topics, from routine maintenance to advanced strategies for engine care, always with a focus on safety and cost-effectiveness.

A closer regional reference is Melvyn Becerra, a fixed-wing and helicopter pilot, instructor, mechanic, and professional chemist. Based in Chile, Becerra continuously shares valuable insights on these topics, demonstrating solid expertise, exceptional technical proficiency, and remarkable teaching skills. The content presented below is derived mainly from Busch's writings and Becerra's lectures.

Both experts highlight that new technologies for monitoring engine parameters, such as individual cylinder monitoring instruments and precise data interpretation, have revealed the possibility of optimizing engine operation. This involves achieving an ideal balance between Exhaust Gas Temperature (EGT), Cylinder Head Temperature (CHT), and Internal Cylinder Pressure (ICP)—the three variables that dictate mixture management. While direct ICP measurement is unavailable, it can be inferred from CHT readings, as their peaks occur under the same mixture configurations.

The use of lean mixtures, known as "Lean of Peak" (LOP), is an advanced technique in piston engine operation that has gained popularity, especially among pilots seeking to maximize fuel efficiency and extend engine life. This practice represents a significant shift from traditional engine operation, which has historically favored the use of rich mixtures (with higher fuel content) as a means to protect the engine and ensure safe operation.

This new technique requires constant monitoring of the engine's condition, with special attention to temperature. However, new monitoring instruments provide better readings and more efficient operation, typically sacrificing some power but granting the engine greater durability and fuel savings.

In the context of LOP, one of the most critical aspects to monitor are the Exhaust Gas Temperatures (EGT) and Cylinder Head Temperatures (CHT). These parameters provide a detailed view of how each engine cylinder is functioning, allowing the pilot to adjust the mixture so that each cylinder operates within safe and efficient ranges.

To achieve effective monitoring, it is essential that the aircraft is equipped with an engine monitoring system that provides real-time data for each cylinder. A modern monitoring system generally includes EGT and CHT probes for each cylinder, allowing the pilot to see how the temperature changes in response to mixture adjustments. This type of system not only shows absolute temperatures but also highlights the trend of change, which is a good indicator for making fine and safe adjustments during flight. This means the ability to anticipate and react to variations in monitoring data to avoid potentially dangerous situations, such as detonation or overheating. If it is observed that the EGT or CHT are approaching upper limits, the pilot can choose to adjust the mixture, reduce power, or change the flight configuration to mitigate the risk.

Monitoring EGT is particularly important because the LOP technique is based on observing when the exhaust gas temperature reaches its peak and how it behaves when adjusting the mixture towards a leaner condition. When the engine is in a rich mixture configuration, the EGT rises until it reaches a peak, and then begins to descend as the mixture is further enriched. In LOP, the pilot adjusts the mixture to pass that peak towards a leaner condition, where the EGT begins to drop again. This descent is a key indicator that the engine is operating in LOP.

However, it's important to understand that not all cylinders reach peak EGT simultaneously. Some may reach it before others, which can result in uneven operation if not properly monitored and adjusted. Therefore, a precise monitoring system should display the temperatures of each cylinder separately, allowing the pilot to identify any discrepancies and adjust the mixture so that all cylinders are operating uniformly.

More importantly, monitoring CHT is crucial, as high temperatures are the most stressful for the engine. While EGT provides information about combustion efficiency, CHT indicates the thermal load each cylinder endures. In LOP conditions, CHT tends to be lower than in rich mixture operations, which is beneficial for engine longevity. However, if the CHT of a particular cylinder is significantly higher than the others, this may signal a problem, such as an unbalanced mixture or a cylinder not operating optimally.

In addition to monitoring EGT and CHT, it's equally important to pay attention to other engine indicators, such as fuel pressure, oil pressure, and engine RPM. These parameters can offer additional clues about how the engine is functioning and whether the adjustments made are within a safe range.

A critical aspect of precise monitoring is the ability to correctly interpret the data and make real-time adjustments. This requires the pilot to not only be familiar with the operation of the monitoring system but also to have a deep understanding of how this data relates to engine behavior under different mixture conditions. For example, an experienced pilot will know that a sudden drop in a cylinder's CHT, without a corresponding change in the others, could indicate a problem that needs immediate attention.

Precise engine monitoring is not just a useful tool but an absolute necessity when operating in Lean of Peak. It allows pilots to maximize fuel efficiency and engine longevity while maintaining safe and controlled operation. Equipping the aircraft with an adequate monitoring system and developing the skill to interpret and act upon the provided data are essential steps for any pilot wishing to fully leverage the LOP technique.

The essence of LOP lies in adjusting the air-fuel mixture to a point where the air proportion is greater than necessary to reach the peak exhaust gas temperature (EGT). In a piston engine, when the mixture is leaned beyond this peak point, the temperature begins to decrease, and it is precisely in this operating zone where the engine can function more efficiently in terms of fuel consumption. However, this approach is not simply a matter of reducing fuel flow; it requires detailed engine knowledge, precise monitoring, and rigorous maintenance.

One of the most attractive aspects of operating Lean of Peak (LOP) is the reduction in fuel consumption. During extended cruise flights, this technique allows pilots to save a significant amount of fuel, which not only lowers operational costs but also increases the aircraft's range. From a technical perspective, operating in LOP mode means the engine runs on less fuel, reducing carbon buildup on key components such as spark plugs and valves. This positively impacts engine longevity, decreasing the frequency of required maintenance and, consequently, lowering long-term costs.

In addition to fuel efficiency, operating in LOP has direct implications for the engine's internal temperature. Contrary to intuitive assumptions, a leaner mixture reduces cylinder temperatures because combustion occurs more slowly and generates less energy per unit of time. When properly adjusted, an engine running in LOP mode can operate cooler, reducing the risk of overheating and the associated stress on internal engine components. This additional cooling also lowers the risk of pre-ignition or detonation, undesirable conditions that can cause severe engine damage.

However, the use of LOP is not suitable for all engines and should not be practiced without proper preparation and equipment. It is essential that the engine is in optimal maintenance condition, including a clean fuel injection system and well-maintained spark plugs. Additionally, detailed monitoring equipment is indispensable, allowing the pilot to observe exhaust gas temperatures (EGT) and cylinder head temperatures (CHT) for each cylinder. This ensures that all cylinders operate within safe ranges and that none are experiencing adverse conditions that could lead to engine failure.

Implementing LOP also requires a precise understanding of how the engine responds to different mixture settings. The pilot must adjust the mixture gradually and carefully, monitoring changes in exhaust gas and cylinder head temperatures, and ensuring that all cylinders are operating uniformly and within safe parameters. This technique demands constant vigilance and a deep understanding of the engine and its behavior, making it a practice that, while beneficial, is not suitable for everyone.

One of the primary concerns when operating in Lean of Peak (LOP) mode is the possibility that not all cylinders will reach their optimal LOP point simultaneously. This lack of uniformity can result in some cylinders operating under non-ideal conditions, leading to uneven performance and potentially hazardous situations. For this reason, effectively practicing LOP requires the pilot to identify and address any discrepancies in cylinder performance, adjusting the mixture and other parameters as needed to ensure safe operation.

Using a lean mixture, or LOP, is a technique that offers significant benefits in terms of fuel efficiency and engine longevity but is best suited for extended cruise phases. In mountain flying, it is crucial to consider that operating a piston engine using the Lean of Peak technique results in a power loss compared to operating in Rich of Peak (ROP) mode. This power reduction is a natural consequence of the lower fuel content in the air-fuel mixture.

The exact amount of power loss can vary depending on the specific engine and the altitude at which the aircraft is flying. However, as a general rule, a power reduction of approximately 10% to 15% can be expected when compared to ROP operation.

FLIGHT OF TWO OR MORE AIRCRAFT

Flying in formation with two or more aircraft in mountainous terrain requires meticulous pre-flight planning and precise execution to ensure safety.

During our mountain flying clinics, held in Cholila under the direction of Juan Martín "Tinti" Escobar and Sebastián Jelusic, each day began with detailed theoretical sessions. These sessions addressed not only the technical aspects of mountain flying but also group flying strategies. Following this preparation, we conducted practical flights, allowing participants to apply what they had learned in a controlled environment.

These practical sessions always included a lead aircraft that guided the flight over pre-established circuits. The presence of this guide aircraft provided not only instructional value but also significant reassurance to pilots venturing into mountainous areas for the first time. The lead pilot, with experience in the region and familiarity with the circuits, served as a visual and technical reference, instilling confidence in less experienced participants.

For these group flights, all pilots were trained in formation flying techniques. Although the separation between aircraft was greater than usual for safety reasons, the fundamental principles of formation flying remained intact. Each pilot was taught to understand their position and role within the formation. Visual coordination and communication were deemed essential: all aircraft had to maintain constant contact, remain within sight of each other, and adhere to the rules outlined in the pre-flight briefing, which detailed objectives, routes, and emergency procedures.

The lead pilot bears significant responsibility during these flights, carefully considering airspace constraints, altitude variations, and the maneuvering space required for all aircraft to move safely. The lead pilot sets the speed slightly below cruising levels, ensuring all pilots have additional power reserves to adjust their position in case they fall behind.

Group flights should be conducted over broad valleys, where the ample space and altitude provide a greater margin for maneuvering and reaction time in case of contingencies.

In tighter settings, such as narrow valleys or areas with close mountain ranges, the complexity increases. In such scenarios, formations are often reduced to just two aircraft: the lead and an escort. In this configuration, the escort pilot must rely on the experience and terrain knowledge of the lead pilot, who is responsible for plotting a safe route through the mountainous area.

To optimize visibility and maneuverability, the escort aircraft positions itself slightly to the side and behind the lead aircraft, never directly behind.

It must always remain visible and avoid entering the propeller's slipstream, which could affect its control. This positioning also allows the escort to keep the lead aircraft consistently in sight, maintain a relatively comfortable position, and anticipate its maneuvers, ensuring a safe separation. Additionally, it is crucial for the less experienced pilot to have the most space, which often requires the lead pilot to fly closer to the valley's slope on one side.

This type of flight fosters an atmosphere of trust and learning, where novice pilots can solidify their knowledge and skills in mountain flying while instructors deliver direct and practical guidance. Through these experiences, pilots build confidence in their abilities to face the challenges of mountain flying, learning to coordinate effectively and adapt to the dynamic and demanding nature of mountainous landscapes.

FORCED LANDING OR ACCIDENT IN THE MOUNTAINS

- Forced Landing or Accident in the Mountains
- A forced landing in the mountains with a single-engine aircraft is a situation no pilot is immune to, especially when flying such aircraft.
- As with any emergency landing, the goal is to minimize the ground contact speed—without stalling. Maintaining a controlled airspeed is critical; the objective is to land, not crash.
- With regular practice, pilots develop the habit of constantly scanning for potential emergency landing sites. For frequent routes, these spots should be documented along with their potential usability.
- Although mountainous terrain is generally unsuitable for emergency landings, some areas are more forgiving, such as small marshes, riverbanks, stream edges, or lakeshores. In other cases, the pilot must choose the least traumatic option, where the aircraft may suffer damage, but the priority is always to protect the pilot, crew, and passengers.
- An engine failure in a single-engine aircraft rules out precautionary landings. Almost any terrain can be survivable for a forced landing if the pilot knows how to use the aircraft's structure for protection. The vital structures—cabin and cockpit area—must remain intact. The wings, landing gear, and lower fuselage should be used to absorb the energy of the impact. Body contact with the interior should be minimized by using seat belts and shoulder harnesses. If time permits, any available padding, such as extra clothing,

blankets, or pillows, should be utilized.

- During landing, materials that absorb energy, such as small trees, shrubs, dense vegetation, deep snow, or artificial structures like fences, should be used to dissipate the energy. For instance, if striking a tree is inevitable, it's preferable to hit it with a wing.
- A body of water may often appear as an attractive option, offering a level surface that can absorb the impact to some extent. However, it's important to note that the aircraft may overturn, particularly if equipped with conventional landing gear. Additionally, even if a successful water landing is achieved, the pilot must be prepared to exit the aircraft quickly and swim, often in very cold waters.
- However, in most cases, with proper operation and a reasonably good glide time, it is possible to find a location where damage and impacts are inevitable, but survival is highly likely.
- The following outlines the recommended procedures in the event of experiencing this contingency:
- Once the aircraft has come to a stop, exit quickly to ensure there is no fire hazard. Wait for the engine to cool down if there is spilled fuel.
- Activate the ELT (Emergency Locator Transmitter). If a forced landing is unavoidable, it can often be activated manually before the flight ends, anticipating potential incapacity after the aircraft stops or in case the impact is insufficient to trigger the device automatically.
- Assess the physical condition of all onboard passengers and proceed accordingly. Use the first aid

kit to treat injuries or fractures, which are among the most likely scenarios.

- Check the condition of radio equipment and batteries, and activate emergency systems.
- Protection against the cold is important. Assess the possibility of starting a fire and preparing hot beverages. Additionally, the smoke from the fire can assist rescue teams in locating the crash site.
- After addressing immediate needs, try to rest and think objectively about the possible alternatives without rushing. Anxiety can become a significant obstacle.
- Evaluate the surroundings and set up a camp. If the aircraft is intact, its fuselage can be used as shelter. Prepare for protection against wind and rain.
- Access to water is usually not an issue. The Patagonian Andes have numerous continuous streams from glacial melt. However, water availability is an important consideration.
- Assess and inventory available food supplies. If necessary, find food in the area. If survival equipment includes fishing gear, trout are likely to be present nearby, as they have colonized habitats across the mountain range, even at higher elevations.
- Attempt to establish your geographical position to communicate it if possible.
- Document the event, recording all pertinent information that might aid in subsequent accident investigations.

- Stay close to the aircraft, as it is more visible than a person. The aircraft can also serve as shelter, signaling aid, reflective components, and a storage area for fuel and supplies. Abandon the aircraft only if:
- You receive instructions to do so, possibly to relocate to a designated rescue area.
- You are familiar with the region and certain you can reach nearby shelter, food, or better rescue opportunities.
- After waiting several days, you are convinced that rescue is unlikely.
- If you decide to leave the aircraft, ensure your physical condition is suitable for a long journey and that you have adequate supplies of clothing and food. In this case, leave the following information behind:
- a. Direction to be taken.
- b. Plan to be followed.
- c. All information that could assist a potential rescue team in locating you quickly.

COMMON CAUSES OF ACCIDENTS

1. Adverse Weather Conditions: Rapidly changing mountain climates can reduce visibility, affect aircraft performance, and create challenging flight conditions.

2. Loss of Control Due to Turbulence: Uneven terrain and wind action generate severe turbulence, potentially causing structural damage, destabilization, and risk of control loss.

3. Lack of Familiarity with Terrain: Underestimating the difficulties posed by unfamiliar terrain can lead to poor judgment or an inability to make quick and correct decisions.

4. Errors in Aircraft Performance Calculation: Single-engine aircraft experience reduced performance at high altitudes. Reduced air density can impair climb capacity, maneuverability, and power to overcome elevations or critical situations.

5. Inadequate Emergency Preparedness: Lack of training, experience, and readiness to handle mountain emergencies can exacerbate accident consequences.

6. Loss of Visibility Due to Spatial Disorientation: Mountain visibility can be affected by clouds, fog, or snow, causing spatial disorientation when the pilot lacks clear horizon or terrain references.

7. Mechanical Failures or Engine Malfunctions: Engine failures in single-engine aircraft during mountain flights are critical.

Cold, humidity, altitude, and fuel quality can impact engine performance.

8. Pilot Fatigue and Stress: Mountain flying demands high mental and physical effort. Fatigue or stress from complex maneuvers and sustained concentration can lead to errors in judgment and decision-making.

9. Inadequate Flight Planning: Poor flight planning, including miscalculating flight distance, fuel requirements, and alternate landing options, can lead to emergencies. This includes neglecting weather changes along the route.

10. Each of these factors, alone or in combination, significantly increases the risk of an accident. Preparation, training, and experience are essential for safe mountain flying.

SURVIVAL KIT

1. When flying over remote and hard-to-access areas, there is always a possibility that an emergency could turn into a prolonged survival challenge. Harsh terrain, extreme temperatures, and total isolation demand a well-thought-out onboard survival kit designed for such contingencies.
2. A survival kit is much more than a collection of useful items; it is a critical safety measure that enables the pilot to safeguard their life, stay secure, remain visible, and maintain control of the situation while awaiting rescue. Survival is not only about being located—it also means staying safe and enduring the environment until help arrives. Moreover, the kit provides a sense of autonomy, and knowing you have the necessary tools to face environmental challenges instills confidence, control, and calm, reducing the likelihood of panic—an essential factor for maintaining the self-control required to survive.
3. Modern technology has produced lightweight, high-quality items that can fit into a small, well-organized backpack with multiple compartments. A backpack, unlike a bag or box, is more comfortable to carry.
4. Below is a detailed description of a standard survival kit that does not significantly increase payload weight and is tailored based on accumulated experience from Patagonian pilots, Alaskan bush pilots, mountaineers, and qualified rescue teams from the region.
5. - Sleeping Bag Designed for Sub-Zero Temperatures. Hypothermia is the greatest threat in these situations.

Signal mirror

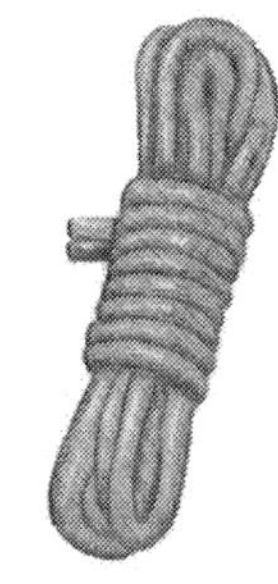

Orange waterproof cloth

Solar charger

Thin and strong rope

Flashlight

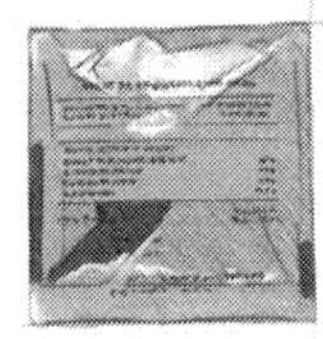

First aid kit

Sleeping bag

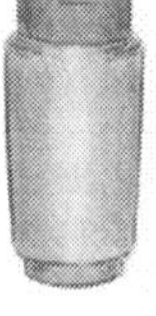

Lighter

Compass

Multifunction tool

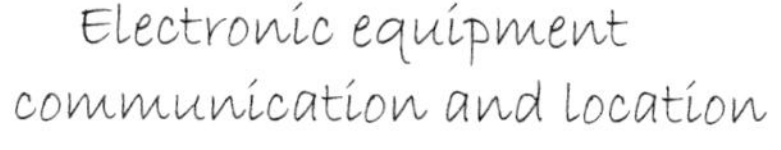

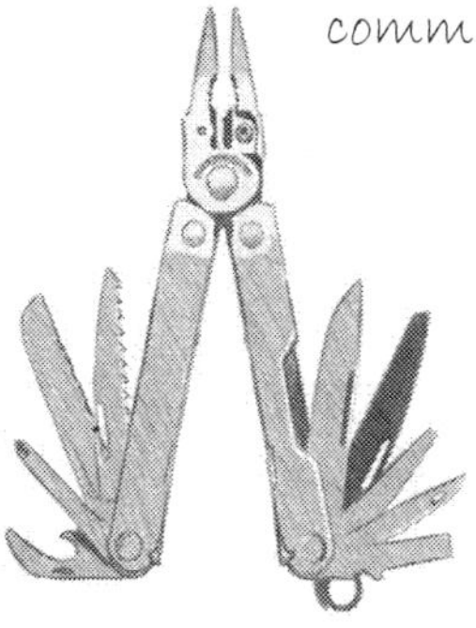

Thermal blanket

Energy and dehydrated foods

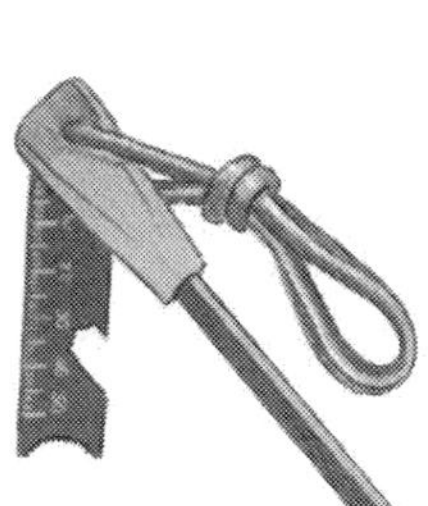

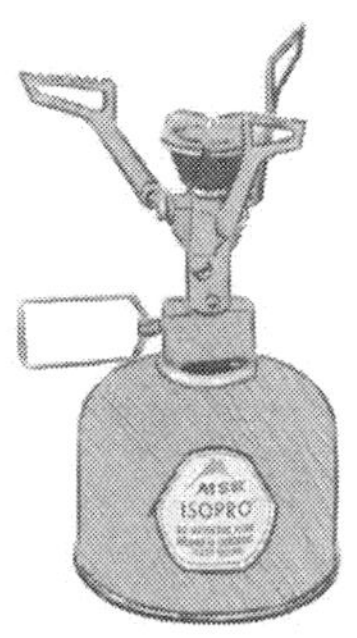

Flint to make fire

Heater

A sub-zero-rated sleeping bag can be used not only for sleeping at night but also for thermal protection during extreme daytime conditions.

6. - Lightweight Emergency Tent. The tent should be wind- and snow-resistant and preferably in a high-visibility color (orange or red) to aid in being spotted. In many cases, a tarp may replace the tent, as it takes up less space while still being large enough to construct a bivouac shelter and provide protection from rain and wind.
7. - Emergency Thermal Blanket. These aluminized blankets, a relatively recent innovation, retain up to 90% of body heat and are extremely compact. They can serve not only as a heat source but also as light reflectors to send distress signals. Additionally, when placed on the ground in an improvised shelter, they create an insulating barrier.
8. - Thin, Durable Rope. Useful for a variety of purposes, such as securing shelters, hanging food to protect it from animals, or even as a fishing line in extreme situations. In emergencies, the inner fibers can be extracted to make fine bindings or repair equipment.
9. - Bush Knife. Large enough to cut wood, clear terrain, craft improvised tools like stakes, and build temporary shelters.
10. - Fire Starters (Lighters, Waterproof Matches, and Flint). Multiple methods for starting a fire, essential for combating cold, heating food or liquids, and producing smoke as a signal for rescuers.
11. - First Aid Kit. A mandatory item for any aircraft, the kit should include gauze, bandages, adhesive

tape, antiseptics, and materials for treating wounds and fractures. Compression bandages and items for emergency sutures are valuable for more severe injuries. Scissors, tweezers, and a scalpel are indispensable for treating wounds, removing splinters, and cutting clothing or bandages. In extreme cases, a scalpel can be used for small incisions, while scissors can modify improvised materials. Additional medications such as painkillers, anti-inflammatories, and antibiotics (in capsules or creams) are critical for preventing infections in open wounds.

12. - Navigation and Signaling Tools. A topographic map and compass as backups in case electronic devices fail. A small, portable, waterproof GPS device can provide precise coordinates to a rescue team if communication is established.
13. - VHF Radio. While these radios have moderate range, they can guide nearby rescue patrols or aircraft conducting search operations.
14. - Signal Mirror. Highly reflective signal mirrors are especially useful during daylight to capture the attention of aircraft or rescue teams.
15. - Electronic Location or Communication Devices. Personal Locator Beacon (PLB): One of the most effective devices for signaling an emergency. When activated, it transmits a distress signal that includes the user's exact location using integrated GPS technology.
16. - Satellite Communication Device. Devices like In Reach allow for two-way messaging and other functions via satellite.
17. - Satellite Phones: Offer global coverage, even from

remote locations like Antarctica.

18. - LED Flashlight. A powerful flashlight is essential for navigating in darkness and sending intermittent signals. To maintain device functionality, carry a small solar panel with the appropriate cables for recharging cell phones, GPS devices, or the flashlight itself.
19. - Small Heater with a Gas Canister. Useful for generating heat in cold conditions, cooking, or boiling water.
20. - Metal Enamel or Aluminum Cup. Durable and heat-resistant, ideal for preparing hot beverages or collecting water from springs.
21. - Food and Water Supplies. Always carry some chocolate bars, hard candies, and energy bars. Include long-lasting, calorie-dense foods. Freeze-dried options are lightweight and require only hot water. Pack dehydrated soup sachets, tea bags, or instant coffee.
22. - A Change of Lightweight Thermal Clothing. Protected against moisture, this should include a jumpsuit, pants, socks, thermal gloves, and a hat.
23. - Flight Clothing. Whenever possible, wear warm, waterproof clothing. Footwear should also be water-resistant and suitable for rugged terrain.
24. - Multi-Tool: A versatile tool for cutting rope, preparing food, carving wood, and performing equipment repairs. It can also serve as a means of self-defense and for other survival tasks.
25. - Fishing Kit and Foldable Small-Caliber Rifle. In prolonged survival scenarios, fishing or hunting small animals may be necessary to supplement nutrition and ensure adequate protein intake to prevent weakness.
26. - Thin, Sturdy Wire. A small roll of wire can be used to

secure structures or set up hunting traps.

27. - Small Notebook and Pencil. Essential for recording coordinates, important events, leaving notes, and documenting the situation overall.

THE SAR SERVICE

The primary goal of the SAR (Search and Rescue) service is to organize and coordinate the efforts and resources of various entities—both governmental and private, terrestrial, aerial, and maritime—for the search and rescue of individuals in danger or involved in accidents. This includes rescuing people, crews, and materials, as well as collaborating with other emergency systems and conducting operations through the Rescue Coordination Centers (RCC) within designated areas of responsibility.

The success of SAR operations largely depends on the speed of response and effective coordination among the various stakeholders involved.

Depending on the type of incident, Aeronautical, Maritime, or Terrestrial SAR operations may be activated, with the participation of different organizations as appropriate. Responsibility for terrestrial events falls under provincial security ministries, as in the case of search and rescue missions for hikers, climbers, skiers, or other activities within that domain.

For maritime, lacustrine, or fluvial incidents, responsibility is assigned to the Argentine Navy under Law 22445, except when an aircraft is involved. In such cases, Aeronautical SAR takes over. Aeronautical SAR also handles all incidents involving aircraft, regardless of location.

Since its establishment in Argentina in 1947, Aeronautical SAR was managed by the Air Force until 2007, when non-military aviation activities were transferred to civil jurisdiction. Responsibility was then handed to ANAC (National Civil Aviation Administration). Later, with the creation of EANA (Empresa Argentina de Navegación Aérea), this responsibility was transferred once again and is now managed by EANA.

To standardize and coordinate actions among countries and to share operational guidelines, the International Aeronautical and Maritime Search and Rescue Manual (IAMSAR) serves as a foundational resource. It is designed to standardize and guide SAR operations in maritime and aeronautical environments.

This manual consists of three volumes:

Volume 1: Organization and Management of Search and Rescue Systems

Focuses on the planning and administration of SAR systems. It provides guidelines for establishing, improving, and managing search and rescue systems, including defining resources, policies, organizational structure, and responsibilities of member states and local authorities. The aim is to ensure efficient planning and coordination of SAR operations within their respective jurisdictions and to establish a general framework for international cooperation in rescue operations.

olume 2 focuses on the Coordination and Mission of Search and Rescue Operations.

This volume is aimed at SAR coordinators and response teams, detailing the procedures for the effective execution of SAR missions. It addresses the real-time coordination of operations, the use of SAR equipment and technology, the designation of search areas, localization methods, and rescue techniques. It is a practical and technical resource intended for those directly involved in executing rescue missions, including communication and onsite logistics.

Volume 3 serves as a Guide for Mobile Operators.

This volume is designed to guide crews and mobile operators, such as aircraft and vessels, participating in SAR operations. It includes practical guidelines and checklists for field crews, assisting them in locating and rescuing survivors, as well as in communicating with SAR centers. Additionally, it provides survival techniques for individuals in extreme conditions and offers rescue guidelines for emergencies on land and water.

The National Civil Aviation Administration (ANAC) is the authority responsible for regulating, overseeing, and supervising the SAR service in Argentina. ANAC ensures that SAR operations comply with national and international regulations in alignment with ICAO standards. This oversight guarantees that SAR services adhere to the highest standards of safety and efficiency.

The Argentine Air Navigation Company (EANA S.E.), a state-owned entity, is tasked with providing the SAR service, including the planning and management of aeronautical SAR operations in Argentina. Its role encompasses supervision, communication, and coordination of search and rescue missions, as well as initial medical assistance or medical evacuation in emergencies. EANA S.E. employs both public and private resources, including aircraft, ships, and other facilities that contribute to SAR operations.

To regulate and oversee EANA as the SAR service provider, ANAC utilizes the RAAC 212, which provides a comprehensive framework covering all aspects of the Search and Rescue Service—from organization and coordination to oversight and regulation. This framework ensures effective planning and execution of operations to address air emergencies.

Additionally, ANAC relies on key documents such as:

Annex 12: Dedicated specifically to search and rescue.

The Caribbean and South American Air Navigation Plan (Document 8733): Outlining regional SAR strategies.

Document 7030: Addressing Regional Supplementary Procedures.

The IAMSAR Manual: Described earlier, which provides global standards for SAR operations.

These regulations and resources collectively ensure an organized and effective response to emergencies involving aircraft, maintaining consistency with international standards.

These documents detail the procedures for initiating and executing SAR operations.

This includes everything from receiving alerts about aeronautical emergencies to planning and carrying out search and rescue missions. These procedures ensure an organized and effective response in emergency situations.

The Alert Service, crucial for SAR activation, is typically provided by Air Traffic Service Units. These units are responsible for identifying and declaring an aircraft in an emergency phase and for receiving and managing information related to potential risk situations.

Aviation is inherently a global activity that transcends national borders, making international cooperation a vital component of the SAR system. Part 212 of the RAAC acknowledges this reality and establishes guidelines for collaboration with other countries and international organizations in the execution of search and rescue operations.

Argentina is a signatory to several international agreements regulating SAR cooperation. These agreements provide a framework for mutual assistance between countries when an aircraft in distress crosses national borders or when local resources are insufficient for a successful SAR operation.

In practice, this cooperation can involve real-time information sharing, mobilizing resources and rescue teams from other countries, and jointly participating in complex operations that require coordination among multiple agencies and governments. Argentina also participates in international SAR exercises to ensure that the procedures and technologies used are compatible globally.

To facilitate coordination among nations, jurisdictional regions have been established. These regions do not imply sovereignty but rather assign responsibility for providing the SAR service. All such regions, known as Search and Rescue Regions (SRRs), are defined by ICAO. Each country determines how to organize and structure its SAR service within its assigned region.

Argentina's SRR covers the entire territory of the Republic of Argentina and extends eastward, beneath Uruguay, to approximately the midpoint of the Atlantic Ocean, bordering the jurisdiction assigned to South Africa.

The entire operational process of SAR missions is managed by the Aeronautical Search and Rescue Coordination Center (ARCC). Located at Ezeiza International Airport, the ARCC plans, coordinates, and directs the actions of various resources involved in SAR operations. These resources may include air, land, and sea assets from the armed forces, security agencies, air transport companies, and other public and private organizations.

The operational organization of SAR (Search and Rescue) establishes that, under the authority of the ARCC (Aeronautical Rescue Coordination Center), permanent Aeronautical Search and Rescue Subcenters (ARSC) are located according to the geography and climate of the regions they cover, whose boundaries align with the Flight Information Regions (FIR). These subcenters are responsible for managing SAR operations within their respective areas.

These Subcenters are located in Resistencia, Córdoba, Mendoza, and Comodoro Rivadavia. Both the Coordinating Center and the Subcenters must maintain up-to-date information on available resources in the area, both human and material, their technical capacity, as well as the availability of airstrips, ports, roads, fuel supply, and a thorough understanding of the local geography.

When adequate resources, trained personnel, and timely and correct decisions are in place, procedures follow the detailed steps below.

If the flight is controlled, the information the Coordinating Center receives about an aircraft in distress comes directly from an Air Traffic Control Service. In this case, a flight plan is available, detailing the type of aircraft, endurance, operator, estimated times, souls on board, and other data that facilitate activation and search operations. By submitting the flight plan, the pilot accesses a service that monitors the route and estimated arrivals. While communication is maintained, this plan can be modified in flight.

If arrival does not occur within the expected timeframe and tolerance, there is a lack of communication, or information is received that the aircraft is in danger, this control service will notify SAR, and the Coordinating Center will assess, according to the phases of emergency, whether the service should be activated.

If the flight is uncontrolled, the information reaches SAR through more indirect means, and activation usually takes longer. This often happens when an aircraft takes off from a LAD (Limited Aerodrome) or an air club without air traffic control services. Notification of the situation may come from calls from acquaintances or family members concerned that the aircraft has not arrived within the expected timeframe, and usually, the local police or fire department are first informed, passing the information to the appropriate centers.

Phases of Emergency

The concept of emergency phases in aviation is a structured classification of procedures and response levels for situations where the safety of an aircraft is uncertain or at risk. These phases enable air traffic controllers, rescue teams, and aviation authorities to organize their response progressively and proportionally to the severity of the situation.

Each emergency phase – uncertainty, alert, and distress – represents an increasing level of concern and reaction to the lack of contact or indications of trouble with an aircraft. The process begins with basic attempts to communicate and locate the aircraft, escalating to search procedures, and in extreme cases, full mobilization of rescue teams to save lives and recover the aircraft.

This system helps to prevent premature or insufficient reactions and optimizes coordination among the various organizations involved, providing a common framework to effectively manage any situation that endangers aviation safety.

INCERFA or Uncertainty Phase: This phase is declared when no communication has been received from the aircraft 30 minutes after the expected time, or when it has not arrived at its destination 30 minutes after the scheduled time, but there is no concrete reason to believe it is in danger. During this phase, additional attempts are made to communicate with the crew through all available frequencies, including contacting other aircraft in the same area. Flight plans are reviewed, and operators are contacted for more information about the aircraft and its crew. If contact is not reestablished or the situation worsens, the process moves to the next phase.

ALERFA or Alert Phase: This elevated state of alert is declared if communication attempts continue to fail, or if the aircraft has been reported to have serious issues, or if it has been cleared to land and has not done so within five minutes. This intermediate state is activated when initial indications suggest that something might be wrong, but the situation has not yet escalated to a critical emergency, and it is not assumed that the aircraft is in imminent danger.

During the ALERFA phase, efforts focus on intensifying communication with the missing aircraft. All available frequencies are used, and other aircraft in the area are asked to attempt contact. Simultaneously, all available information is thoroughly reviewed: the flight plan, the aircraft's last known position, weather reports along the route, and any prior communications from the pilots. This detailed analysis may provide clues about what might have gone wrong.

The ALERFA phase also involves the preventive mobilization of resources. Although rescue teams are not immediately deployed, search and rescue units are put on alert, preparing for a rapid response if the situation worsens. Other aircraft may be requested to stand by for SAR (Search and Rescue) support, as well as vessels or ground teams trained and equipped for such tasks. This phase can also involve coordination with other countries if the aircraft is on an international route or near borders, ensuring a joint response if necessary.

All of this occurs while the situation is continuously monitored, maintaining a vigilant attitude and updating the status with any new information that arises.

The ALERFA phase concludes when contact with the aircraft is reestablished, confirming it is not in danger, or when it is confirmed to have landed safely, even if at an unplanned location. However, if at any point evidence emerges that the aircraft is in actual danger, the situation can escalate quickly to the next phase.

DETRESFA or Distress Phase: This phase is activated when the situation becomes critical, and it is recognized that an aircraft is in imminent danger or has suffered an accident. This is the highest level of alert in aeronautical emergency procedures and signals the initiation of an immediate and coordinated response for search and rescue.

The escalation to DETRESFA occurs when signals and information gathered during the earlier phases, particularly during the ALERFA phase, indicate that the aircraft is in a grave situation. For example, if continuous communication attempts fail, the aircraft does not appear on radar, and its estimated arrival time and tolerance have passed. The sudden disappearance of an aircraft from radar without prior warning is one of the clearest signs that something has gone very wrong.

Another situation triggering DETRESFA is the reception of an emergency signal emitted by the Emergency Locator Transmitter (ELT). Similarly, reports from witnesses or other aircraft that have observed the aircraft in trouble—such as a rapid descent or an in-flight fire—are taken as justification to initiate this phase.

DETRESFA is also declared when an aircraft reports severe problems, such as catastrophic engine failure, fuel loss, or extreme weather conditions, and then loses contact. In these cases, the combination of prior reports and subsequent loss of communication leads authorities to assume the aircraft is in imminent danger. Additionally, DETRESFA is activated when the elapsed time indicates that the aircraft has run out of fuel without having landed or communicated its status.

The DETRESFA phase represents a situation of utmost urgency in which the speed of response can make the difference between life and death. Escalation procedures are designed to ensure that resources are mobilized as quickly as possible when an aircraft is suspected to be in danger, minimizing risks and the potential consequences of the emergency.

Once the protocol is activated, the Coordinating Center assumes responsibility for the operation. This center, which may be operated by aeronautical, military, or civil defense authorities depending on the region, begins by evaluating all available information. Based on this assessment, it proceeds to mobilize the necessary resources. These may include search aircraft equipped with radar technology and infrared cameras, helicopters, ground teams specialized in mountain rescue, search dogs, and, in some cases, specialists trained for extreme conditions such as avalanches or glacier rescues.

Planning the search areas is one of the most critical aspects of the operation. In mountainous regions, where the terrain can be extremely rugged and weather conditions can change rapidly, it is essential to establish clear priorities. Rescuers must evaluate the aircraft's planned flight routes and consider factors such as air currents, known turbulence in the region, and the possible presence of natural obstacles that could have forced an emergency landing. Aerial searches are often the first step in the operation. Aircraft and helicopters fly over priority areas, using advanced sensors to detect any signs of the crashed aircraft. However, the effectiveness of aerial searches can be limited by altitude, adverse weather conditions such as low clouds or storms, and the nature of the terrain, which can conceal an aircraft from view.

When aerial searches yield no conclusive results, or when a possible location is identified that requires closer inspection, ground rescue teams are deployed. These teams, made up of trained personnel often experienced in mountaineering or high-altitude rescues, travel on foot or with all-terrain vehicles to reach the location. In many cases, accessing the crash site can be extremely challenging, and rescuers must contend with steep terrain, ice, deep snow, or unstable rocks. The risk of avalanches, landslides, or unstable glaciers is a significant concern in these scenarios. Moreover, teams must be prepared to operate at high altitudes, where the lack of oxygen and extreme temperatures can endanger both rescuers and potential survivors.

Once the aircraft has been located, the next step is to assess the situation. This involves determining the extent of damage to the plane, the condition of any survivors, and the safety of the site. Rescue teams provide first aid and stabilize the injured before planning their evacuation. In a mountainous environment, evacuation can be particularly challenging. In some cases, helicopters can perform a vertical extraction if conditions allow, but in others, a prolonged ground rescue may be necessary, which can take several hours or even days, depending on the distance and terrain conditions.

After the evacuation, survivors are transported to medical facilities where they receive the necessary treatment. Psychological support is also provided to them and their families, who endured the anguish of waiting during the search operations. But the process does not end there. A thorough investigation is subsequently conducted to determine the causes of the accident, which is critical not only for understanding what went wrong but also for improving safety protocols and prevention measures in future operations.

The mountainous environment adds an additional layer of complexity to search and rescue operations. Mountains not only present difficult and often inaccessible terrain but are also subject to rapid and unpredictable weather changes that can seriously complicate operations. Detailed knowledge of the topography, local climate, and human physiology under stress must be considered for a successful operation. Rescuers must be prepared to face extremely low temperatures, altitudes that challenge physical and mental endurance, and an environment where every decision can make the difference between success and failure.

Each operation is unique, and although the basic principles of rescue remain the same, tactics and strategies must be adapted to the specific circumstances of each accident. The combination of preparation, coordination, and experience is ultimately what makes it possible to save lives in one of the most hostile environments a pilot can encounter.

NEW TECHNOLOGIES AVAILABLE FOR AVIATION

In the modern world of aviation, pilots have access to a variety of tools and technologies that assist with navigation in mountainous terrain. Beyond detailed topographic maps, advanced GPS systems and digital platforms enable the planning of safe routes and the avoidance of obstacles.

Many of these digital systems are free to use, available in web, desktop, and mobile versions, making them accessible across a wide range of devices and suitable for different contexts and purposes. These tools are valuable for learning, satisfying curiosity, or addressing the real need to plan a flight. They allow users to chart routes and evaluate terrain elevations through simulated flight perspectives.

With these applications, it is possible to visualize any corner of the planet with remarkable precision, whether in two or three dimensions. One of their most impressive features is the ability to view landscapes in 3D, offering an immersive experience when virtually exploring mountainous regions.

This is further enhanced by information layers that add details about roads, borders, points of interest, as well as historical and demographic data, enriching the exploration experience.

In emergencies, much of this technology is applicable and is complemented by specific tools designed to facilitate search efforts.

ELT (Emergency Locator Transmitter)

When a notification is received indicating that an aircraft may have crashed in a mountainous area, the first step is the immediate activation of the emergency protocol. This notification can originate from various sources, one of the most common being the automatic activation of the Emergency Locator Transmitter (ELT), which emits a signal to satellites upon detecting a significant impact.

The ELT operates by initiating its signal either automatically or manually. Automatic activation occurs when the device detects a sudden deceleration, such as during an impact. This deceleration is registered by a G-force switch, which activates the ELT when a preset threshold is exceeded. In addition to automatic activation, pilots or crew members can manually activate the device, either after landing or preemptively if an imminent emergency is anticipated. This ensures that the ELT is triggered even if the impact incapacitates the crew from taking action.

Once activated, the ELT begins transmitting signals on various radio frequencies. Traditionally, these signals were transmitted at 121.5 MHz and 243.0 MHz, frequencies that were widely monitored. However, with technological advancements, these frequencies have gradually been replaced by the 406 MHz frequency, which offers significant advantages. ELTs operating at 406 MHz not only produce a more accurate and robust signal but also transmit encoded data about the aircraft, including type, registration, and country of registry, as well as details such as color, owner, and a contact phone number. In some cases, they may even include the last known position, which is extremely useful for rescue teams in their localization and assistance efforts.

The signal transmitted at 406 MHz is picked up by the Cospas-Sarsat satellite constellation, which is specifically designed for the detection and localization of distress signals. This system employs satellites in different orbital types to ensure global coverage. Among these are low-Earth orbit satellites, known as LEOs, operating at altitudes between 800 and 1,000 kilometers above the Earth. Their low altitude allows them to pass quickly and repeatedly over the same area, facilitating frequent updates on the distress signal's position. These satellites can detect emergency signals using the Doppler effect, enabling them to calculate the approximate position of the transmitter. The effect is observed as follows: if the satellite is approaching the transmitter, the frequency received increases as the radio waves "compress." Conversely, if the satellite is moving away from the beacon, the signal frequency decreases as the radio waves "expand" with distance.

In addition to low-Earth orbit satellites, the Cospas-Sarsat system also employs geostationary satellites, known as GEOs. These satellites operate at approximately 36,000 kilometers above the Earth, allowing them to remain in a fixed position relative to a specific point on the Earth's surface, providing continuous coverage in their visibility area. However, unlike LEO satellites, GEO satellites cannot determine the signal's position using the Doppler effect, so their primary function is to detect signals and retransmit them to ground stations.

Lastly, the Cospas-Sarsat system has incorporated an additional layer of medium-Earth orbit satellites, known as MEOs. These satellites operate at altitudes of approximately 20,000 kilometers and combine the advantages of LEO and GEO satellites, providing both rapid and continuous coverage, as well as improved capabilities for locating emergency signals. Examples of MEO satellites in this network include the European Union's Galileo constellation and the United States' GPS satellites.

The duration of an ELT's signal transmission is also a critical consideration. These devices are designed to operate for at least 24 to 48 hours, depending on the model and battery capacity. However, the ELT system has its limitations. In extremely remote areas or those with complex terrain, such as mountains or deep canyons, the ELT signal may be obstructed, complicating detection. Moreover, while the 406 MHz technology has improved location accuracy, precision can still vary, with a general accuracy range between 2 and 5 kilometers.

The ELT requires regular maintenance to ensure its

functionality in case of an emergency. It is essential to conduct periodic inspections and functionality tests to ensure the device is in perfect working condition, particularly the battery, which must be ready to operate when needed most.

In Argentina, as in many other countries, the installation and operation of an ELT is mandatory for most civil aircraft. This requirement is established by the National Civil Aviation Administration (ANAC), following the international standards set by the International Civil Aviation Organization (ICAO). Regulations specify that all Argentine-registered aircraft conducting international flights must be equipped with an ELT operating at 406 MHz. For domestic flights, most general aviation, commercial, and transport aircraft are also required to have this device, with some exceptions for certain categories, such as ultralight aircraft or those used exclusively for local flights.

Linked to SAR, there are twenty-four Mission Control Centers (MCC) worldwide, one of which is located in Argentina at the Palomar Air Force Base. It is jointly managed by the Argentine Air Force and Navy. This center, known as the Argentine Mission Control Center (ARMCC), receives information via space and terrestrial technologies and relays it to the Search and Rescue Coordination Center, which verifies the information and decides on resource deployment.

Satellite Tracking Systems

Satellite tracking systems, such as SPOT and Garmin inReach, enable real-time tracking of aircraft via portable devices that transmit their location through satellite networks. These systems are particularly useful in remote areas where radio or cellular coverage is nonexistent. In emergency situations, pilots can send distress messages with their exact location, facilitating a swift response from rescue teams.

ADS-B (Automatic Dependent Surveillance-Broadcast)

ADS-B is a technology that allows aircraft to transmit their position, altitude, speed, and other data via radio signals. These data are received by ground stations and other ADS-B-equipped aircraft, providing a real-time view of air traffic. In emergencies, ADS-B data can be used to track the last known position of an aircraft. Furthermore, the implementation of ADS-B Out is becoming a mandatory requirement in many regions worldwide, thereby increasing coverage and the effectiveness of tracking.

Drones for Search and Rescue

Drones have become valuable tools in search and rescue operations, particularly in challenging or inaccessible terrains. Equipped with high-resolution cameras, thermal sensors, and autonomous flight capabilities, drones can cover large areas quickly, searching for signs of life or aircraft wreckage. In mountainous or forested regions, drones allow rescue teams to inspect hazardous areas without risking human lives.

Radar and LIDAR

(Light Detection and Ranging) technologies are sometimes used to detect aircraft in hard-to-reach areas. Radar can be mounted on aircraft or ground stations to track moving objects, even in low-visibility conditions. LIDAR, on the other hand, uses laser pulses to create detailed three-dimensional maps of the terrain, which can be helpful in identifying aircraft debris in forested or mountainous regions.

Communication Technology

Effective communication is critical during search and rescue operations. Rescue teams use VHF/UHF radios and satellite communication systems such as Iridium and Inmarsat to coordinate operations in real time, especially in areas where traditional communication infrastructure is limited.

Mobile Applications and Navigation Software

Mobile applications and aviation-specific navigation software provide tools for pilots to plan flights, track their position in real time, and send alerts in case of deviations or emergencies. These systems, connected to tracking and communication devices, can be crucial for quick localization in the event of an accident.

Coordinated Search and Rescue Fleets

Some search and rescue organizations have developed coordinated fleets of light aircraft equipped with advanced technologies for rescue missions. These fleets may include airplanes and helicopters outfitted with sensors, cameras, and state-of-the-art communication systems, capable of operating in extreme conditions.

Artificial Intelligence and Data Analysis

Artificial Intelligence (AI) and advanced data analytics are beginning to play a significant role in search and rescue operations. Systems that process large volumes of data from satellites, sensors, and other sources can predict patterns and suggest priority search areas, enhancing the efficiency of rescue missions.

SAFETY RULES IN THE MOUNTAIN PILOT

Being a prudent pilot in the context of mountain flying involves adhering to certain fundamental principles. These axioms serve as a foundation to mitigate the inherent risks of this type of flying.

These principles are simple guidelines to enhance safety in the high mountain environment, where a small mistake can have significant consequences. Prudence in mountain flying is based on proper preparation, constant evaluation of the situation, and a deep respect for the conditions and rugged terrain.

Among others:

1. Know your limits and the aircraft's

Before embarking on any mountain flight, it is essential to know and respect the aircraft's capabilities and be aware of your own skill level. Objectively assessing personal limitations in terms of experience, training, and physical ability is as important as understanding the aircraft's specifications and limitations, such as power, glide ratio, climb rate, high-altitude performance, and response to turbulence.

2. Planning and foresight

This includes analyzing weather conditions, evaluating routes, and preparing alternative "escape" routes. Knowing what possible changes in the weather could occur and anticipating the risks of being caught in marginal conditions, determining and evaluating the most reliable route with maps or electronic means, considering high elevations, available emergency landing zones, and escape options in very adverse situations, will provide a margin of safety for this type of flying. In mountainous areas, weather can change quickly, so it is essential to have a safety margin.

Having an alternative route is crucial in the mountains. Each segment should be planned with a safe exit in case something doesn't go as expected, whether due to adverse weather conditions, technical failures, or unexpected situations. Knowing where to land or return can make the difference between an adventure and an accident.

3. Adaptation to the environment

Prudence in mountain flying requires an adaptable attitude. Maintaining flexibility in plans is necessary, as the pilot may face unforeseen situations that make the planned route unfeasible. Being ready to alter the route, abort a crossing, or even turn back is a sign of wisdom and prudence.

4. Always fly with margins

- When approaching a ridge or peak, position and altitude are critical. The "ridge effect" refers to the intense updrafts and downdrafts generated at these points, which can destabilize the aircraft. Always maintaining a safe altitude and staying clear of ridges is a prudent measure, as is estimating distances with additional safety margins.

5. Make decisions based on data, not emotions

- In mountain flying, emotional reactions can affect decision-making. Fatigue, tiredness, and frustration are common in these conditions. A prudent pilot knows how to identify these emotional states and avoid them, keeping focus on the data and logic rather than being swayed by emotions.

6. Maintain a continuous learning attitude

- A prudent pilot never stops learning. Accumulated experience doesn't mean abandoning curiosity or humility. In mountain flying, every experience offers lessons. Analyzing each flight, discussing with other pilots, and continuously improving knowledge about the terrain and its peculiarities strengthens preparation and skill.

7. Follow these general rules to reduce risks

- Do not fly in mountainous areas without a minimum of 150 hours of flying experience, which is the estimated number for most flying activities requiring some practice.

- Do not allow a passenger to pressure you into starting the flight if weather conditions are not safe or if there is doubt about the aircraft's performance.

- Do not plan a cross-country flight to the mountains when the wind at the mountaintop exceeds 25 knots, unless you have experience with operations in strong updrafts, downdrafts, and moderate or greater turbulence. This recommendation does not exclude the possibility of an exploratory flight.

- Avoid routes that do not provide a suitable area for an emergency landing.

- Do not fly in the mountains with an unfamiliar aircraft model or brand.

- Do not operate low-performance aircraft on marginal mountain runways.

- Do not rely on cloud shadows to determine wind direction. Depending on the topography, the wind at lower altitudes may likely be in a different direction and very changeable.

- Do not reduce speed in a downdraft. If you maintain speed, you will be under the influence of the current for a shorter period, and you will lose less altitude overall.

- Do not underestimate the adverse effect of frost. A light frost significantly affects airflow over the wings, reducing lift and increasing drag.

- Do not neglect the importance of fuel and survival equipment. It is important to keep the aircraft light, but do not skimp on these items. Plan the fuel load to allow for the flight from the departure airport to the destination with a reserve to handle unexpected winds.

- Do not fly through canyons. This puts you in a bad position for making a turn. Always ensure an escape route.

- Do not spare efforts in seeking information from maps, electronic means, and other local or experienced pilots.

- Do not rely too much on the horizon when flying with an external visual reference. A gently sloping terrain may cause a visual distortion. The horizon is the base of the mountains.

- Do not cross ridges perpendicularly. Approach should be made at an angle, preferably 45 degrees when you are between half a mile and a quarter mile away. This allows for an escape with less stress for both the pilot and the aircraft if unexpected situations arise.

- Never disregard common sense when flying in the mountains. If there are any adverse conditions that compromise the operation, cancel or postpone the flight until the situation improves.

EPILOGUE

By Günter Schuster

This book is not just a narrative; it is a testament to courage, resilience, and learning. It is a work that inspires, instructs, and above all, imparts a profound lesson on what it means to face the unknown with determination. Through its pages, we are guided on a journey where the inherent dangers of flying in remote mountainous areas take on an extraordinary dimension. These regions, difficult to access, pose a challenge even to the most experienced pilots and their aircraft, designed to operate in extreme conditions but not always fully adaptable to the complexity of the environment.

Queque's experience is something no one would wish to face, not even in the most controlled training scenarios. Yet, it happened. What follows is a story of survival and resilience that leaves an indelible mark on those who learn of it. His rescue was the result of a confluence of factors: physical and mental preparation, timely decisions, and, above all, the tireless spirit of those who worked relentlessly to recover him. This account vividly demonstrates the fragility of the human being when confronted with a formidable nature capable of testing the innermost limits of our existence.

This book also clearly underscores a critical lesson: the importance of flying accompanied during such operations. The presence of another aircraft and at least two or more crew members not only adds an extra margin of safety but also provides invaluable support for observation, decision-making, and assistance in critical situations. This principle, so fundamental in mountain aviation, is reinforced time and again in the story that Daniel shares with wisdom and generosity.

Daniel, the author and protagonist of this book, not only

documents the events and takes part in the search and rescue, but also provides invaluable insight into the challenges of flying in the Patagonian Andes—one of the most majestic and at the same time unpredictable regions on the planet. His words are imbued with practical advice, technical recommendations, and a profound love for aviation and nature. However, he also confronts us with a troubling reality: the insufficiency of rescue equipment for operations of this kind. This deficit not only exposes pilots and rescuers to additional risks but also underscores the need to approach the planning of such missions with greater rigor.

The meteorological phenomena described in these pages are not mere secondary details; they are actors in a story that highlights the constant and often unpredictable variability of mountain conditions. Under these circumstances, Queque's attitude stands out exceptionally. His ability to overcome physical and mental challenges, even in the harshest conditions, is a testament to his character and training. It was this fortitude that allowed him to endure with the limited supplies Daniel, piloting his reliable Cessna 180, managed to deliver on two critical occasions, facing the pressure of the approaching nightfall.

For Daniel and Pablo, seeing their friend walking near the wrecked plane was a moment filled with mixed emotions: relief, disbelief, and renewed determination. However, this moment did not mark the end of the story. Over a frozen lake, where the ice's strength was uncertain, they made the right decision to drop basic supplies that could mean the difference between life and death for Queque during the freezing night ahead. This act of commitment reflects the essence of what it means to be a general aviation pilot: being willing to go beyond personal limits to support and protect others.

What this book describes transcends a technical operation or a physical endurance act. It is a tribute to the general aviation community, a community united by a shared passion for flight and an unwavering commitment to the safety and well-being of others. Through its pages, Daniel shows us how the passion for flying can become a transformative force, capable of inspiring others and profoundly impacting the lives of those who share this love for the skies.

In this epilogue, I want to express my deepest gratitude and recognition to all the people who participated in Queque's rescue. Their dedication, sacrifice, and humanity not only saved a life but also reminded us of the power of teamwork and the strength of solidarity. May this book be an inspiration to all those who find in flight not just a profession but a way of life and a bridge to the extraordinary.

My most sincere gratitude and admiration go to Queque, Daniel, Pablo, and all those who made this memorable adventure possible. May their experiences continue to illuminate the paths of those who, like them, live with their eyes set on the clouds and their hearts filled with determination.

BIBLIOGRAPHY

- Anderson, Fletcher. 2003. Flying the Mountains: A Training Manual for Flying Single-Engine Aircraft 1st Edición. Ed. Mc Graw Hill, 332 pp.
- Auxier, Eric. 2012. The last Bush pilots. Independent Publishing Platform, 306 pp.
- Busch, Mike. 2018. Mike Busch on Engines: What Every Aircraft Owner Needs to Know about the Design, Operation, Condition Monitoring, Maintenance and Troubleshooting of Piston Aircraft Engines. Ed. Savvy Aviation, 508 pp.
- Comando General de la Fuerza Aérea. Dirección de Tránsito Aéreo. Manual de Operaciones. Procedimientos de Búsqueda y Salvamento.
- Comando de Institutos Aeronáuticos militares. Escuela de Aviación militar. 1951. Manual de Pilotaje. Aeronáutica Argentina. 100 pp.
- Comando de Regiones Aéreas. Dirección de Fomento y Habilitación. Manual Experimental de vuelo. Industria Gráfica de Aeronáutica.
- Comando en Jefe de la Fuerza Aérea Argentina. Manual del instructor de vuelo. Dirección de Aviación Civil.
- Dirección General de Circulación Aérea y Aeródromos. 1966. Manual de Supervivencia. Búsqueda y Salvamento. Aeronáutica Argentina. 120 pp.
- Hoover Amy & Dick Williams. 2019. Mountain, Canyon, and Backcountry Flying. Ed. Aviation Supplies & Academics, Incorporated, 392 pp.

- Imeson, Sparky. 2001. Mountain Flying Bible & Flight Operations Handbook Expanded. Ed. Aurora Publications, 512 pp.
- Lynn, Wyatt. 2017. Memories from my Logbook. A Bush Pilot's Story. Ed. Booklocker.com, Incorporated, 144 pp.
- Mason, Mort. 2017. WHAT IT'S REALLY LIKE: FLYING THE ALASKA BUSH. Ed. Kindle, 307 pp.
- Mock, Jerrie. 2014. Three-Eight Charlie. Ed. Phoenix Graphix Publishing Services LLC, 274 pp.
- Montejano, Bernardino. 2017. Saint Exupéry, jardinero de hombres. Ed Distal, 452 pp.
- Organización de Aviación Civil Internacional. 2004. Búsqueda y Salvamento. Anexo 12.
- U.S. Department of Transportation Federal Aviation Administration. TIPS on MOUNTAIN FLYING. FAA Aviation Safety Program. Washington, D.C. 17 PP.
- Pocock, M. C. C. 2017. Bush & Mountain Flying: A Comprehensive Guide to Advanced Bush & Mountain Flying. Ed. Digital Publishing of Florida, Incorporated.
- Civil Aviation Authority of New Zealand. 2021. Mountain flying. 36 pp.
- Cessna 180 Owners Manual. Cessna Aircraft Company. Wichita, Kansas USA. 1955. 92 pp.

Made in the USA
Columbia, SC
24 January 2025

5a108212-b02e-43b1-8faa-3b8d863cc8e4R01